T0354628

THE
IMMIGRANT

MIREK MAZUR

BALBOA.PRESS

A DIVISION OF HAY HOUSE

Balboa Press books may be ordered through booksellers or by contacting:

Balboa Press
A Division of Hay House
1663 Liberty Drive
Bloomington, IN 47403
www.balboapress.com
844-682-1282

Because of the dynamic nature of the Internet, any web addresses or
links contained in this book may have changed since publication and
may no longer be valid. The views expressed in this work are solely those
of the author and do not necessarily reflect the views of the publisher,
and the publisher hereby disclaims any responsibility for them.

The author of this book does not dispense medical advice or prescribe the use
of any technique as a form of treatment for physical, emotional, or medical
problems without the advice of a physician, either directly or indirectly. The
intent of the author is only to offer information of a general nature to help
you in your quest for emotional and spiritual well-being. In the event you use
any of the information in this book for yourself, which is your constitutional
right, the author and the publisher assume no responsibility for your actions.

Any people depicted in stock imagery provided by Getty Images are
models, and such images are being used for illustrative purposes only.
Certain stock imagery © Getty Images.

Print information available on the last page.

ISBN: 979-8-7652-3271-2 (sc)
ISBN: 979-8-7652-3270-5 (hc)
ISBN: 979-8-7652-3476-1 (e)

Library of Congress Control Number: 2022917317

Balboa Press rev. date: 10/06/2022

Contents

Introduction

I was dead before I was born. My journey started in 1960. At a young age, my mother got pregnant but she was not so lucky as her fetus was forming outside her uterus and she required immediate surgery. This was a very risky and life threatening procedure in 1960 in communist Poland. However the procedure went well and my mother survived, with a big scar across her stomach. Not so many weeks later she received both good and bad news from the doctor; she was pregnant again. The bad news was her body had not yet fully recovered from the surgery and the doctors recommended an abortion since she wouldn't survive the pregnancy. The doctors simply said she had a 95 percent chance of dying from complications.

My mother was always a feisty woman. Years earlier she prevented one of the local communist leaders from repossessing her house and property. My father could not help because in those days a man standing up to the police risked being sent to jail. So it was all up to my mother to fight.

After three months of eviction notices, the police came and tried to force themselves through the doors that my mother had blocked with everything she could. Her only weapons were pickle jars, the most Polish things ever. In the meantime, she sent a letter to the radio station FALLA49, which was in Warsaw and connected to the government. In three days, she got a response from Communist Headquarters that she could keep the house and she would be left alone. The same letter went to city hall and the local communist party office. Because of her persistence, she was able to keep her house. Most people would have given up. But not her. That same stubbornness is why my mother chose to continue her pregnancy with me rather than terminate as was recommended. I was born in the depths of winter in that very same house. It's beautiful symmetry, when you think about it.

Now, it was not a perfect beginning for me. Let's say it was not a happy start to my life. Soon after my birth I developed a viral infection; and for the first 12 days I cried in hospital with inflamed testicles. I was pumped with antibiotics and medications. At the end the doctors told my parents that most likely I would never be able to have children. My mother only shared this information with me many years later after my son Peter was born. She figured if I knew that, I would never have tried to have a child. A very smart lady.

If you live in a big city, you have most certainly seen people crossing the street carrying bags of groceries. Maybe they are wearing exotic clothing such as saris or turban. Maybe they have a turban on, or head covering. Maybe they are wearing warm-up suits that are not sold in Canada. They seem foreign to you. They may not fit in, you think. They are walking with their shopping as they cannot afford a car. They have little money but are doing what they need to survive. One of those people could well be your future mechanic, teacher, doctor or boss. They may have fled a distant country to start a new life for themselves in a new country. Many immigrants in Canada start their new lives this way. I know this because I immigrated to Canada many years ago. I had nothing but hopes, dreams and the hunger to be successful in my new life.

1

An immigrant survives on little but hope. Immigrating is not an easy thing, but it's even more complicated when you're a refugee who has left home with no money and your only language is your mother tongue.

The first time I ever heard the word "migration" was when I was a child. My teacher talked about birds migrating south to Africa at the end of summer. Then they came back in the spring, as a long-awaited sign of the end of winter.

Years later I found out my paternal grandfather traveled to America in the 1920s. He went there for a better life. There were no planes in those days, so he took a ship like so many others. His uncle found him a job in Chicago. He returned to Poland after just three years and was able to purchase a big plot of land with a river running through it, which powered a water mill. He had a very nice property and raised his seven children there until World War Two changed everything.

Before the Second World War, in a general sense, Poland was peaceful and tolerant compared to many other European nations. At that time, there were more Jews in Poland than in all of Europe mainly due to Poland's progressive tolerance. There was antisemitism all over Europe, of course, but less so in my home country, which is why more Jewish people lived in Poland than all of Europe. Of course, all that changed after, sadly, but it is important to point out that Poland was unlike some of its neighbors.

After the war, my mother at nine years old and her family were forced to move from the Polish side of Ukraine to Poland to avoid slaughter and genocide. When the war ended, my family spread to other parts of Europe including Italy and France. My uncle met his French wife and an aunt met her Italian husband in labor camps and they moved to those other countries after the war.

Postwar, Poland became part of the Soviet Union which of course explained why so many would never be able to or want to come back. During Communism, Poland was, in a way, the best place in the worst system. It is hard to say why Poland ended up as the only country in the communist bloc where people could experience so much freedom, but this was the case. When I was a child growing up in Poland, me and my family members could travel to other countries as long as we showed them that we had money. And speaking of money, in Poland there were special stores where you could buy all sorts of things from other countries if you had American dollars, including American blue jeans.

The other thing that was different in Poland during communist times was that Polish people were not cut off from other peoples' cultures like in the USSR. I studied French and British writers, read American books, and watched American movies. In Poland we could watch the latest films at the theaters, and often some of the best and current rock groups came to Poland for concerts.

Perhaps that was the reason for the first successful uprisings that started in Poland in the eighties. Polish people were well aware of freedom outside of the Iron Curtain and did their best to fight for at least a comparable amount of the same. Poland had one of the first constitutions in the world and even though it was now part of the Soviet Union, Poles enjoyed a small amount of sovereignty. Slavery never existed in Poland and never would. It was just the mentality of the nation that had been developed for hundreds of years.

One of the first books I read as a young boy was *The Prairie* by James Cooper. It was about a trapper who moves to the plains to escape the growth of houses and factories as cities stretch farther and farther west. In my eyes, it was a beautifully written book that opened my mind. I realize now that it very much started my immigration dream, the romantic idea of moving and settling down. Occasionally I'd be reminded of that book many years later when I was driving across the prairies of North America, thinking about how hard life must have been for the first immigrants traveling by horse in that new land of hope.

People immigrate for different reasons, but most of the time it is to escape oppression or poverty. I made a decision to find my purpose in life, to find my own destiny, that didn't involve someone telling me what to do. But I was under no romantic delusions, I had no wishful dreaming. I simply wanted to start a new life in the New World.

What made up my mind was my first trip to Italy with my mother (Bronislawa) and my cousin Ted. He was one of my most interesting relatives who had traveled all over the world. He worked as a teacher and was very cosmopolitan. I had cousins all over Europe and we were allowed to visit family— as long as we promised to return to Poland. I know now if I had not visited my family at the age of twelve in Italy, I would never have left Poland for good only eight years later. I know that trip was a life-changing one. I was impressed with the great food, style, beauty and romance. Of course, in order to enjoy this type of lifestyle in reality, one needs to work hard and land a good job.

I made the decision to leave Poland a long time before I left. My first chance was at age eighteen. I developed a friendship with an Italian girl. She invited me for two weeks of skiing in the Alps. Her parents would cover all the costs once I arrived; I just had to buy the plane ticket to Italy. I don't know if it was destiny or bad luck. Just as the school winter break was beginning and I was set to travel, an epic winter storm descended over Europe. It wasn't just any storm, it was the storm of the century. Everything was shut down, trains, planes and all transportation. I was stuck and unable to go. All my plans to ski, to go to Italy, were thrown in the trash. I was so disappointed that I decided then and there I didn't want to live in Poland anymore. It's almost like Mother Nature didn't like me and wanted to complicate my life. But I knew I had to be persistent. Nothing would stop me in the future.

In my youth I was a professional cyclist. At the end of the season when I was twenty years of age, I was selected by my cycling club to race the last international stage race in October. It was very cold and very tough. At one stage, it was so cold I could not feel my feet. It was a multi-day race and very challenging. Although I was frozen and miserable, I knew I had to give it everything I had. I got in the breakaway group and completely buried myself, pushing the biggest gear the entire time. When I finished, I felt a weird soreness in my foot, but I didn't think it was a big deal. It turns out I split my muscle that day, by pushing so hard in the brutal weather.

I was in a cast for three months; my foot was severely injured. I couldn't walk at first. I was in so much pain. Despite getting paid by my club, I made a decision to stop my career as an athlete. The injury changed me. Had I never had that injury, my life would never have gone the way it did. Life throws opportunities at you and sometimes you only realize them later in life. When one door closes, another opens.

At age twenty, it was almost impossible to leave Poland. Serving in the army was mandatory at that time, and only doing sports kept me away from military service. I made a chance and made a decision to at least try. I went to apply for a passport at the police station. The actual application was straightforward but additional requirements I was never aware of made me realize it was going to be a difficult process. I was worried and nervous that

I would never be permitted to leave Poland. To get a passport, I needed permission from my workplace, the army and a final stamp from the local police station. I had to prove I had over $200 to my name so I would not embarrass Poland and the Soviet Union by becoming homeless and begging for money in a foreign country.

Since I quit my job as a pro athlete, I needed to get a stamp from an employer. Thankfully, my cousin had a car-painting business and he hired me. I had to show I worked for over a year but I only worked there a few weeks. Good thing my cousin was starting to be very influential in town; he managed to pull some strings and got my papers stamped at the labor office. Thanks to my cousin and his white lie, I was closer to my goal of emigrating.

Next I drove to the nearest army base in the next town to procure my stamp. I was on the list to start my two to three years of army service in special forces. I was scared because I had never been on a base before. It was very intimidating being surrounded with big walls, like a proper army base. I walked into an imposing old building and was directed to an office on the second floor. At the doors, this tall officer ushered me into a very large office. I walked in and there was an officer sitting at the desk- with a nice haircut, slim, very fit, in his '40s. I sat down and he looked at me and started to go through my files. He said, "So what do you want to do?" I said, "well, I'd like to go visit my family in Italy. And I need a stamp". He opened my documents, looked at my name, looked at me and smiled. He said "You're Mazur?", I replied "yes", nervously. And he smiled at me again and asked if I was from my town Jelcz. He gave me the stamp and he returned my documents to me and I said, "thank you very much" and "Goodbye". Later, he phoned my mother and he said, "You know your son was here." He told her I was a very lucky man as it just happened that he was sitting in for the regular person in charge of applications. If the other officer had been there that day, I would never have got the stamp. The officer recognized my name and remembered me from when I was five years old and at his wedding to my cousin from town. I don't remember of course, but it's another one of those strange little things that happened in life that allowed me to pursue my goal of emigrating.

I assumed incorrectly that the worst stress was behind me since I had all the required documents. However, when I got to the police station to pick up my passport it was evident that something was wrong. An old and fat officer looked over all my documents and then pointed to the stamp from my cousin for proof of employment and stated that this was going to cost me a lot. He said to come back in seven days to see if it had been approved. It was the longest seven days of my life. I could not sleep and I hardly ate. The police in communist Poland were a powerful institution. When I returned seven days later the policeman handed me the passport and said good luck. It was strange at first-after so much stress for seven days and then no issues. Ten years later I found out from my mother that through her connections she had paid a bribe to the fat policeman for the passport. This was very common in communist Poland. The last obstacle to prepare for my future was to make sure my girlfriend could travel as well. Her passport was given to her no problem as she was a university student.

I will never forget the day we boarded the plane to Italy. I was anxious and nervous the whole time. I kept looking down the aisle, wondering if the police would come and drag me off the plane. I had done what I had to, got all my papers but I was freaking out that they would figure something out and detain us. Waiting for the plane to take off felt like an eternity. I was sweating and time stood still. I looked out to the tarmac to see if anyone was coming. Finally, we took off. What a relief it was. All I was thinking was I would never return to Poland.

2

My aunt Stanislawa, had a very hard life in Italy, I won't lie. Shortly after getting married in Italy, she got pregnant. But then her husband died in a car accident. That meant she was not only a mother, but had no husband to help support her in hard times right after the war. She did everything she could to survive, mostly cleaning windows, houses, toilets. She did what she had to do.

When we touched down in Italy, my aunt picked me up in Milan and we stayed with my Italian family in the small town of Revere for two months until we made the decision to enter the refugee camp in Latina, 100 km south of Rome. There were two immigrant camps in Latina funded by UNESCO. We took a train and arrived at the gates of the camp. Then we were escorted by very friendly Italian police. They took our passports a way took all our information and directed us to the office where we were given pillows and blankets.

In those days, if you were not married, you were not allowed to share a room. The camp we were staying at was for singles. Married couples and families with young children were put up in hotels rather than in the camps. The conditions in the camp were deplorable. I was directed to a small room with broken windows that accommodated four single men. The housing was basically barracks and was very rudimentary. Many of the men were criminals and unfriendly. My girlfriend Eva was put up in a large room that was once a gym in the old days. Most of the single women staying there were prostitutes and came from all over Europe. There was very little space to walk between the beds. We were miserable. There was a lot of crime there and all in all, it was a very unpleasant experience. Some of the refugees had escaped from Albania and some of them were criminals. We heard there were some bloody fights in the camps and some people even got murdered. The Italian police did not care. We were treated like animals, but as long as UNESCO kept sending the Italians money, it was all they cared about. For them, the refugee camps were a great business. They earned good money as they got paid per head. In return, the Italians would supply the bare minimum in food and shelter and the money would just keep coming, even if the refugees were living in squalor. It only changed when the Pope came to visit in 1982, due to complaints from Polish people who were at the camp.

We befriended some of the refugee families who felt sorry for us and took us under their wings in their quarters. They strongly suggested that we move out of the camp and into a hotel room in town.

We lasted only seven long days at the camp before we made the decision to rent a hotel room. I had some savings from driving a tractor at a pear orchard when we were staying at my aunt's home. We used that to pay for the hotel as we were not eligible for free accommodation from UNESCO. This prompted us to get married quickly so that we would qualify for the free accommodation outside of the camp reserved for married couples.

We had already applied to emigrate to Australia months before because we didn't want to stay in Italy forever. The problem was there was a recession in Australia so our departure date kept getting postponed. However, we soon learned Canada was more than happy to accept us, so we made a decision to change plans and apply for Canada.

One day we got an appointment with the Canadian consulate in Rome for the final interview which would determine our eligibility. We ended up in a room deep in the consulate, with a big map of Canada hanging behind the desk of the consul. He was a nice man and straightforward. He asked us, a very young couple in our twenties, with our whole lives ahead of us, a simple question: "What would we like to do in Canada?" What a question to ask. I had no idea. And I certainly had no idea what to do in Canada, a country I knew so little about. I looked at the map of Canada and saw a drawing of a man in a checkered jacket, holding an axe: "I want to be a lumberjack." I replay.

He smiled at my answer. His next question was even more daunting: "Where do you want to live in Canada?" I was looking at this big map of a big country. All I asked was where was the warmest place, since we had very little clothing. He pointed to the map and said, Vancouver. So, Vancouver it was.

3

E va and I wanted to get married but we could not afford a church wedding. A big wedding in a church in Poland often continued for up to two days. It was very expensive as you were expected to invite all of the extended family which could be half a village. I come from a large family; my mother and father had seven brothers and sisters. Growing up, I attended a lot of weddings. My mother organized weddings for both of my sisters, Danka and Zdzicha. I remember slaughtering over 20 chickens and numerous turkeys for each of their weddings. I had a big log and a big axe. I had to chop off all of their heads so they could pluck the feathers and prepare different dishes to eat. I was fourteen, but it was my job for my sisters' weddings.

I was not very religious in any case as I'd stopped enjoying church long before. My grandmother used to babysit me and on many occasions she would take me to church when I was five or six. I was mystified by the strange rituals- like my grandmother kissing the local priest's hand while on her knees on the steps of the church. I could never understand why he was putting his hand out to be kissed by an older woman on her knees. So from an early age, I questioned the church and refused to become an altar boy despite it being a big deal in Poland which was very Catholic. So Eva and I married in a government service.

It did not take long after one government wedding in Latina to finally get us a room in Rome in the hotel for married couples paid by UNESCO. It was a great moment to leave the refugee camp in Latina and the hotel that we had to spend money on outside of the refugee camp. In Rome we ended up getting a small room in the hotel on the 10th floor. It was a very old building that had cracks and scars from earthquakes which are very common in Rome. After finding work quite easily, we wasted no time familiarizing ourselves with the local neighborhood and visiting the tourist sites and historic architecture dating back over 2000 years.

One day I received news from back home that one of the girls that attended the same college as me ended up becoming a nun and was working in Rome. After getting her number from my sister, I called to see if we could meet. The last time I'd seen her she was dancing at the school discotheque. She was from my town and her younger sister was at school with me for 12 years, so I knew her sister Josephine well. We arranged to meet one day at the Vatican, in front of the Basilica. After talking about the old days, and bringing up the old memories, Sister Josephine asked if we were married, I said yes. The next question was if we were married in a church.

Right away we learned from Sister Josephine that a wedding is valid only if performed in a Catholic way, in front of God, in a church. A day or two later, the Sister met with us again, excited to share some good news. She and her congregation had decided to organize and arrange a wedding for us in a church. My wife was so happy that my doubts and reservations about the Catholic church disappeared quickly.

Soon we found out it was not going to be in any church but in the Vatican itself. This unnerved me but made my wife very happy. In three weeks the Sister had found a priest, a wedding dress, a driver of a nice Alfa Romeo and organized a big dinner at their congregation.

All of my refugee friends took part in the ceremony although it was strange not having anyone from my family. All went smoothly and at the end of the day we were married again. The reception took place at the Sister's monastery, a new building lined with first class marble, located just outside of Rome. My refugee friends and I went for a drinking party in our hotel at the train station. I drank far too much and was sick to my stomach in the morning.

It was time to get back to reality in Rome but we had great memories and a certificate from the Vatican signed by the Pope for the future.

One month after our wedding at the Vatican, I met someone who would become a good friend. On one of my explorations of the town, I had found a soccer field near the Coliseum. It was hard to believe that this great monument had existed for 2000 years. The soccer field was for locals and could be accessed anytime. it was a good size with slightly smaller nets, which made scoring harder. On one of the game days we ended up playing a hard physical game which was up to my style of play. One player was giving me a hard time to the point that I was planning to beat him up after the game. When the game finished, I started walking towards him and he turned with a smile and asked me which way I was heading. I said, towards the train station. He said he was headed the same way and we could walk together. He introduced himself as Dominic and started to ask me a lot of questions. When I asked what he did for a living, to my surprise, he told me he was a priest from northern Italy, studying his way up the priest hierarchy.

On the way to the hotel we stopped and he began talking to two prostitutes from the street. He did not want to reform them, he was simply being kind. I showed him where I lived and he came back and invited my wife and me for dinner. Many dinners later we found out he was from a rich family that had kindly offered us jobs in the family business. This meant we could stay in Italy permanently which we liked as I had family there and Italy wasn't far from Poland. Unfortunately, we could not apply for Italian citizenship because we were coming from a communist country.

Two weekends a month Dominic traveled to a remote town in Italy called Amelia, to lead Sunday services. On one occasion he asked us to join him for the weekend and as we had nothing planned, we accepted his offer. Amelia was a small walled medieval town atop a mountain in central Italy. The church was very old and was once a seminary with a number of buildings. It sat at the very top of the hill. It was late and very dark when we finally arrived in Amelia. Dominic opened the big heavy door, it was very dark and the first thing we saw were many ready made up beds in what looked like a dormitory. It was a very big room and everything was very clean. It was open to anyone who needed a place to sleep. There was no electricity so we used candles. Soon we reached one of the rooms that looked like a very big kitchen. There was food ready for us, even though it was already 11 pm. There was a heavy table set with white tablecloths, and lots of wine, salami, olives, cheese and bread.

Everything looked superbly clean but at the same time very spooky and cold because of the size of the rooms, the stone, and all the shining candles. We did not know if the three hour drive to Amelia had made us very hungry but the meal was delicious. It was all local food that included hand-made salami. It was the best we ever had. It's hard to describe how good the wine and food made us feel.

Since it was in the mountains and in the old monastery, there was no heat at night and it was very cold. The building was medieval, with old windows that let in the cold air. That's the thing about many of the buildings in the old country; they are hundreds of years old. They are beautiful and impressive but far from modern with very small single beds. After we ate, Dominic showed us to our room. It was on the top floor of the main building and on the top of the mountain with an incredible view of the surrounding countryside. Dominic's room was on the bottom floor. It was a stormy night, with lots of thunder, lightning and wind. Eva and I slept in the same single bed in order to stay warm.

The following day was Sunday and it was time to attend the local church service. We wanted to see Dominic at work. The church was full but he managed to seat us in the front row. He introduced us to the locals which was a little embarrassing. Dominic then announced that all of the money collected from the donations that day would go to us. It was very generous of him as we had very little money. This was the first time we experienced the kindness of charity. These people did not even know us yet were giving us some of their hard earned money. In other people's eyes, we must have seemed quite destitute. In fact, both of us came from good families in Poland and didn't consider ourselves poor.

After church, Dominic took us for a scenic hike up the mountains. At the top, we reached a large imposing abbey with few windows. We were told that once a nun moved into the abbey, she lived a cloistered life and never left or was seen by outsiders. The abbey supported itself in part by selling pasta dinners to passing tourists like us. We put in our order through a small opening in the door and out came three delicious dinners. I can still remember the fresh aromas and flavors-it was the perfect meal for three cold and hungry hikers.

Later that evening we set off on our drive back to Rome. The roads were narrow and winded through the mountains. Eva began feeling sick and proceeded to throw up. This was strange since we had eaten the same foods. Two weeks later we found out Eva was pregnant. God must work in mysterious ways, I guess.

It happened on the bus in Rome. My wife was on her way to work and suddenly felt ill and fainted. An ambulance took her to hospital. Eva was very pale and felt terrible. The doctors at the hospital were rude and disrespectful- laughing that she was not sick but pregnant. She felt very uncomfortable and did not like being touched by these doctors. When Dominic found out about her treatment in the hospital, he was not very happy. He did some research and found Father John, whose job was to translate documents for the Pope. He was a Polish Canadian, the son of Polish immigrants, and it was no surprise that he had connections to important people in town. It just happened he knew the best doctor in Rome. His name was Professor Moneta and he was the director of the main hospital in Rome, the Clinica Gemelli. They took care of my pregnant wife. She got the very best treatment.

It was an incredible experience for us as young refugees to meet the very famous Dr. Moneta. His generosity did not stop there. He invited us to meet his wife and children and it was a little intimidating at the time. He was a real big shot with an incredible house that was hundreds of years old. We spoke Italian the whole time with him, and had a very lovely time. His home was very fancy with amazing decorations, expensive furniture and ornate rugs. In the center of the room was a portrait of his grandfather, Ernesto, who had won the Nobel Peace Prize in 1908. Since we were from communist country, he pulled out letters from Lenin written to his father.

They were a most significant piece of history, those letters. It was surreal to even see handwritten letters by Lenin. At the end of the visit, the wife of Dr. Moneta gave my wife Eva earrings, a bracelet and necklace made of ivory.

Although we were set to emigrate to Canada shortly thereafter, we stayed in touch with Father John and when our son, Peter was born, nine months later we asked Father John to be his godfather. He had class, he not only accepted but flew all the way to Vancouver for the christening.

15

4

Finally the time came to fly to our new destination, not Australia but Canada. We did not own many winter clothes as our original plan was Australia. After our arrival in Montreal, we went through the border checkpoint, and we were taken by bus to a nearby Holiday Inn. We both felt nervous but excited to learn what was coming next for us in the New Country. We didn't have a lot of money in our pockets, and of course we didn't speak the language yet, so as you can imagine, we had a lot on our minds.

At the Holiday Inn we were assigned to our rooms and then after unloading what little luggage we had, we headed to our first meal in Canada. It was an American-style buffet which was totally new to us. There was no such thing in Europe. Tables and tables of all kinds of different foods you could eat. We were both so hungry, but we hardly had any money, so we didn't eat too much. The problem was, we didn't understand that it was all free!

We found out later that we could have eaten so much more food without paying a cent, but by then it was too late. After one night in Montreal, all of us immigrants were separated and directed to our chosen destinations. Of those who were on our initial flight, some would go to Toronto, some would go to Calgary, some to the East Coast, it was wherever they had picked in their own initial meeting with the Canadian consulate. We had chosen Vancouver, so that was where we headed the next day.

The entire trip from Rome was paid for by the Canadian government. I remember we had to sign an agreement saying that we would pay the government back for it some day, but the agreement was largely symbolic. In a way, we did pay for future immigrants like us through our income tax, so I guess it all worked out.

I will never forget landing in the Vancouver airport. It was absolutely breathtaking. We had very good luck with the weather, it was a perfect summer day so we could see the Rocky Mountains covered in snow and of course the Pacific Ocean, right beside the city we would soon call home. I had never seen a more naturally beautiful city from a plane and to this day, I think it is still true. We were landing in the city where we were starting a new chapter in our lives, we were overwhelmed with excitement.

As we approached Vancouver, my wife and I noticed many houses had pools, some even had tennis courts. We were speechless. One of the first things that came out of my mouth was that we will someday own one of those houses with the pool and big backyard.

We were 21 years old with a baby on the way in five months and we were full of energy and hope. We didn't know what to expect, or what the future held for us in this new country.

Two things are important to remember. We were coming from a communist country and we were also very young. We didn't understand some of the aspects of living in a capitalist society. One thing that we had no experience with was an economic recession which was in full swing when we arrived in Canada. No one mentioned at the Canadian consulate that there was a recession in Canada or that unemployment was at 16 per cent. There was little to no work. It had never crossed our minds that we would have trouble finding work. We'd soon find out though.

Once we got off the plane and got our luggage, a car was waiting to drive us to our hotel, the English Bay Inn. Our hotel was at Davis and Denman Street, right at the beach, which was not a bad start. We were told that we could stay there until we could find our own accommodations. After a few days we received some money to buy some food. The other surprise for us was that there was a tax on food! We never had to pay taxes in Poland, and it was something we had to start taking into account when we budgeted our daily expenses.

We started to feel positive about our situation. Vancouver was a beautiful city with clean fresh air from the ocean. We had lots to explore as there was lots of open space. There were still lots of unknowns of course and no family around to help.

After a month in the hotel we found a place to stay; it was an apartment on Cambie Street and Marina Drive, on the 8th floor. The building had a swimming pool and a nice view of the Vancouver International Airport. Further away, across the American border we could see the site of an old volcano, Mount Baker.

At first the apartment building seemed perfect to us, the rent was fair and the owners were Polish immigrants. But we soon found out having no money, no car and expecting a baby wasn't the best way to create friends. We noticed that no one wanted to be friends with us in the building. I decided to look for some friends outside of the apartment building. I signed up for a local Polish soccer team. It had a friendly atmosphere, some of the players were established Polish expats, some were like me, fresh off the boat.

I was born to be a soccer player. I was one of the top prospects in my club in the '70s. My parents never cared what I was doing, they were busy working. Plus, I was much younger than my sisters so I had a lot of freedom. I was born the same year as the first man to go into space, Juri Gagarin, in 1961.

At the age of 12, I signed myself up for the second division soccer club, sponsored by the local factory, Moto-Jelcz. The club was 10 km away but they gave me a monthly bus pass to get to practice.

Everything at my club was top class. Like all top teams in Europe, they had feeder teams with youngsters who would grow up in the club, with the hope they would play on the pro team. We had coaching, free equipment, great facilities and lots of games. I really enjoyed the discipline and professionalism. Everyone at 12 felt like future stars. We'd meet every day during the week for a two hour practice and then we'd have games on Sundays. I was a midfielder from the get- go. After two years I was playing with 18 year old, when I was just 14. I was a very physical player but also very fast. These were very happy days for me despite the bullying I experienced from a group of local boys for a few weeks until I threw one of them down the second floor stairs. After that, everyone was my friend.

After sleeping the first few days on the floor, my wife and I finally got some basic furniture, courtesy of the government. A kitchen table, two chairs, that sort of thing. We also received some money for clothing and basic items for Eva, some baby clothes for when Peter was to arrive and me. All of this was desperately needed to live a normal existence. Soon I started classes to learn English. The classes were eight hours a day five times a week for six months. My wife had to stay home and learn English on her own, as she was expecting our son any day.

It was hard for her to learn a new language on her own, but soon we met Kay Christie: a rich woman who volunteered to teach immigrants English. She was a very nice woman and her help was really appreciated. Her daughter was married to Valdy, a famous Canadian folk singer at the time. We had a chance to meet the Juno award winner at the Kay family Christmas party. He was a nice guy. The Christies had a very nice villa in North Vancouver. Kay not only helped my wife with English, but after getting to know her, instilled such confidence in her, making her feel she could become anything she set her mind to and have a good life in Canada.

At first I did not like the English language. I didn't think I could ever learn it. It was very difficult, even though I had already studied German, Russian and Italian in the past. Slowly it became fun. I was in a class with 15 Chinese people, four Eastern Europeans, and an Indian man. I was the youngest in the class—some of my classmates were well over 40.

Basically, I made school into a fun activity. I think I was learning the fastest, on account of my age, so the day would be spent with me conversing with the teacher, the rest of my class would write it down. That is one of the reasons I never learned to write English well, or spell properly as I was always talking. After six months I passed the final exam and was ready to look for a job.

The apartment building had some negative aspects. Not only was it infested with cockroaches but a lot of the immigrants there had a hard time getting jobs. There was very high unemployment, so many of them settled for welfare. Most of our neighbors were in their 30s and 40s leaving established professions in Poland. It was a tough time for them, given that they had such high hopes in the New Country. Some of them even went back to Poland. Some of them would spend their days drinking. My next door neighbor left his wife, a doctor in Poland, and started having a relationship with the apartment building owner's wife. Some became desperate, wanting a better life for a better future.

Before Peter was even born, my wife was lucky to find a job cleaning houses two to three times a week for extra money, even though she was seven months pregnant. The first year in Canada was very hard, we try to forget those times. I can't imagine how tough it was for Eva.

We used to go shopping for groceries, one and a half kilometers away on Granville street, but we'd walk the whole distance to save a transit fare. Or we'd get supplies at an inexpensive Chinese store in Richmond, walking the long trip with heavy bags on hot days. We had enough money to live off welfare but to save we had to do things like not use the bus to stretch out the payments.

When my wife went into labor, she ended up in a brand new hospital with her own room in Shaughnessy hospital, she even had her own TV! Total luxury. One thing we sometimes do not realize in Canada and we take for granted is that every person is treated the same way with the same access to medical service.

In many countries money gets you the better doctor and better services.

Initially, I didn't want to watch the birth. But ultimately, I was convinced to watch. Oh boy was that a big mistake. It was not a walk in the park by any means. They pulled the kid head out with some big pliers, which made me almost faint. To my big surprise, my son ended up coming out perfectly clean. No blood at all. December 2, 1982 was the best day of my life. My son was born: Peter Gregory Mazur. I'm sure most parents feel the same way when they have children. We had nothing, now we had a baby. We never imagined that a baby could make us so happy. The whole experience inspired us to work harder in our journey.

5

hen I first started my job search it was very confusing. First, I didn't even know *how* to look for a job in Canada. I had never looked for one before. Plus, I didn't even know what I wanted to do, or what I was looking for. And finally— there was a damn recession going on!

Back in Poland I was paid as a professional athlete, my wife was a student. My wife's first job in Italy was in a me*rcato*, cleaning vegetables in frozen water at 5am and paid very poorly. I ended up cleaning dishes in a nice restaurant. But it wasn't like we had so much experience with any skilled jobs, our resumes were a little thin. In Italy, we kept doing those jobs the mercato and the restaurant for very little money, until one day a Polish lady found us. She needed a babysitter so that her 7-year-old daughter could continue to speak Polish during the day and not forget her native language. And, she needed someone to keep her house clean. We moved into their house, just outside of Rome next to the former Italian President Leone house. I got a job in construction from her rich boyfriend who was a developer.

Later I found out he had a wife. The Polish lady was his young mistress. He bought her an expensive house and a cosmetic shop in Rome. He found me a construction job within walking distance of our villa. Finally we started making good money and we had a car to drive, we could eat anything we wished and drink as much wine. The Polish lady was easy going and nice. Sometimes she would ask me if I wanted to have a plate of food and wine in the middle of the night after she got back from parties in Monte Carlo. It was a great life for a while, but did not last very long. We finally got our documents for Canada and had to leave that big house. We left all the money we made in Italy with Father John for safe-keeping, we thought it would be taken from us at the Canadian border.

Anyway, fast forward to Canada and there I was looking for a job, walking on Broadway Street, looking for help, reading signs on both sides of the street, not having much luck. As I walked, I noticed a bike store, the first one I'd seen in Vancouver. To be honest, I was more interested in what bikes they were selling as opposed to a job. I made a decision to go in and look despite only having five dollars in my pocket. The staff was very friendly and made me feel comfortable enough to ask for a job. I was directed to the owner, who was very much into bike racing. After a quick chat, he decided to give me a chance and hire me as a mechanic. I could not wait to get home and tell Eva that I'd landed my first job and was getting paid six dollars an hour. It was not much but at that time in the early 80s you were happy making something as opposed to nothing.

All my Polish welfare friends in the apartment building kept making fun of me and kept discouraging me from working as I could get the same amount from welfare. To me, it wasn't just a job, but an opportunity to meet new people in this new country and chapter of my life. I played soccer on the weekends with the Polish soccer team. We never lost a game. Things were going sort of well, a job, some fun, and a son!

Soon I got my first bike in Canada, a Miyata and I started riding it to work every day. Meanwhile, my wife was making great progress studying English at home with the help of Kay.

In general, most Canadians are very friendly, but there are exceptions. We were young and naïve, and we learned a few life lessons early. One Saturday morning, I opened the door to see a very well-dressed gentleman in a nice suit and tie. He was friendly, and introduced himself. Then he asked us if he could give us a presentation; in return we could get a free gift. So of course, we let him in and he showed us a vacuum cleaner. He told us it was the most powerful vacuum cleaner on the market. It swallowed these big metal balls, and had a lifetime warranty. He was a very convincing salesperson, charismatic and friendly. We were instantly sold on this amazing invention. He just kept feeding us more and more information and we were blown away by how great of a product he was selling.

The fact that we clearly had no money didn't discourage him one bit. He told us we could pay with monthly payments. Wow. It sounded so great. My wife was so impressed with his professionalism and kindness toward poor people she made him sandwiches and coffee. We had 16 square feet of carpet in our apartment, so he said it would be great. It will be great for my son's sake to keep it clean. He was very convincing. We bought the vacuum, and signed the papers for the payment plan with this great man who was so concerned about our son's health. We now had the best vacuum on the market! The next day Kay showed up to help my wife. We told her the great news about the vacuum, The Filter Queen. Kay did not seem quite as excited as we were. She politely asked for the contract that we had signed. After checking all the papers Kay informed us that by the end of the payment we would be paying well over $700 because of hidden costs and interest. On Monday, Kay took our documents and made some calls, managing to reduce our final cost to $500. We paid a high price for a very good lesson that would save us down the road.

On the upside, the vacuum cleaner would last us 20 years. As soon as my wife learned English she started looking for a job that would suit her lifestyle and give her time to be at home with our son. Kay was instrumental in helping my wife write her first resume which was a huge help. My wife started applying for the most suitable job, an apartment building manager. At first the task was almost impossible as her English was still limited. Plus, not only did we have no experience, but we knew we were so young and that we would be judged by that. We made a decision not to reveal our ages, so at least that would give us a foot in the door. All we wanted to do was work.

My wife started applying to every ad in the local Vancouver newspaper. She had two interviews which seemed to go well so we got our hopes up that we would maybe land a job. In reality, we had a hard time imagining someone giving a couple of kids a chance to manage properties. On the day of the interviews we were nervous; they were our first ones in Canada and we didn't know what to expect. We tried to look as good as we could—just like the look of the vacuum salesman. We lied and said we were 28. I am not sure if they bought it, but they liked us and we ended up with two job offers.

The first job was to run an upscale complex, reporting to one supervisor. The second job was in the east end of Vancouver with no supervision and flexible working time. We took the latter; it was less money but it was flexible. Both of us had other commitments, my wife was going to Capilano College. I was a bike mechanic in the store.

6

My cycling career started very early in my life and ended too soon. When I was 15 and a full blown soccer player, a friend in my class, who was also a racer and belonged to the same club, asked me if I could bike. He wondered if I could represent the school in the local championships. The races intended to look for new cycling talent for the local club. I immediately said no, I'd never raced, plus I didn't have a bike. But since I was the most athletic student at the school, he offered to lend me a bike so I could enter the race and give it a try.

The race was an hour long and in the forest on dirt roads. I ended up winning in spite of not knowing much about cycling tactics. I never saw my competition after the start of the race. I had never experienced winning individually. I was a soccer player, in soccer we lost the game but my coach would say after the game that I had played very well. In cycling you only had a good day when you won. That part made me feel good at winning on my own without a team. So, I did not switch clubs, I just switched sports within the club. Four months later, I'd finish fifth in the time trial out of 500 kids at the Polish Summer Games. One year later I was in the medals. The first important thing I learned from an early age was that there is a lot of talent out there and the winner is the rider who leaves more than he has on the road on the given day.

With my job in the bike shop, everything was going well. I started to ride my new bike a few days a week with the owner of the Rocky Mountain Company, Jacob Heilbron. Since I had no money to buy racing gear he gave me some shorts, jerseys and old shoes. I wasn't saying much when we rode, I was always worried about my grammar. I was very quiet then. So one of the reasons that people didn't know much about me and my past was because I was worried about my English. After riding a couple of times with the local group I started to get stronger again. The owner noticed that I was getting pretty strong, so we started to talk more about my past in cycling. I told him how I raced in Poland. He asked me to ride for the Rocky Mountain team, but at the time there was no money for riding bike. I had to decline, I had a baby and I needed to make a living, not just ride for free equipment. Remember, in Poland when we raced for the club we got a salary and equipment, not to mention a mechanic and massage therapy.

One day at the bike shop a Polish boy named Wojtek showed up looking for a bike to start as a bike courier in downtown Vancouver. The bike salesman asked if I could speak with Wojtek since I spoke Polish. Wojtek told me he used to race in Poland and wanted to start racing in Canada. He asked me if there was a bike shop which would give him free bikes and clothing. I told him that I will try to asked Jacob if he could sponsor the new kid from Poland. Sure enough, the owner gave him a Guerciotti bike and some clothing. This made me feel good to be able to help someone I barely knew.

Soon, Wojtek asked me to help with his training program as he didn't know where to start. It was Fall, so cyclo-cross was about to start. He rode eight hours a day as a courier, so that was a good start. What he needed was some specific training, stuff like intervals four times a week. We practiced dismounting over obstacles, running up the hills, all the things you need to be a fast cyclo-cross rider. He would become the provincial cyclo-cross champion that year. He was the first person I ever coached.

I know now, and knew then, we immigrants all had to do what we had to to survive. We had to bend the truth a little to get ahead, to open doors. I was only a few years older than the boy from Poland, but he had no family in Canada, and I became one of his few friends. He was my first champion ever, all my efforts and time paid off and it felt very rewarding succeeding at something in the new country.

After over a year of working at a bike shop, things were not working out with the new store manager. I was let go. I never found out the reason why, I never had complaints from customers as far as I knew. I was making good money doing piece work. I was getting paid to take apart bikes, clean factory grease and put in new fresh grease. I was doing seven to eight bikes a day for the three bike shops in Vancouver and at the end of the day my hands were so sore I had to put them in ice cold water to recover for the next day of work. My only problem, maybe, was I was too fast. Before me there were five guys doing the same job, and often the mechanic had to adjust their work to make bikes work perfectly before they were sold. It was good money. I was getting paid $15-20 a bike, working six days a week. The mechanic got paid by the hour--$10, no matter how fast he worked. Maybe the new manager didn't like that the laborer was getting paid more than most people in the store.

Toward the end of my tenure there, my manager started giving me a hard time about how I didn't socialize with my co-workers. He started to make my job less and less enjoyable, trying to make me clean toilets and stuff like that. Now, apart from the fact that I didn't really want to clean toilets, it was also unfair as I was not on salary, I was paid by each bike I would fix. So by sending me to clean toilets, it meant less time to actually earn money. I was furious about that. It was totally unfair.

Looking back, he did me a big favor, I knew I would never try to be a bike mechanic again. Sometimes, things happen for a reason, only time will tell. At that point, it seemed like my story was just about to begin.

Jacob, the owner of the Rocky Mountain company, felt sorry for me and bad about the whole situation. He could not change the mind of the store manager. I was about to go home that day. That was my last day, so I was cleaning up my bench, packing up my tools, when Jacob approached me. He asked me to come to his office in the warehouse at the back of the store. He looked me right in the eye and said: "Mirek, you are going to be a coach."

7

I was a bit surprised, to say the least. The first thing out of my mouth was: "but I've never coached before Wojtek!" I had no coaching credentials, and considered myself way too young at 23 to be a coach.

All he said was there was a very successful Polish coach in the USA named Eddy B. You're Polish, you could do in Canada what he is doing in the USA. Eddy Borysewicz was one of the most well-known American coaches and developed many of the most talented riders down there including Greg LeMond. Despite Eddy B being very well-known and respected in the States, I had never heard of him. I had no clue who this coach was. Later in life me and Eddy B. became friends and my son stayed at his house in Ramona, California for winter training.

At the time I didn't know Jacob was working as a volunteer at Cycling BC as the President and on the board of directors. So, quite instantly and serendipitously, I became both the Cycling BC coach, and the Rocky Mountain coach. Literally overnight.

Some days later I was introduced to the BC board of directors and they sent me to take the Level 1 and 2 courses so I could be a certified coach. Cycling BC paid for me, which was a relief as I probably could not have afforded them. I don't think everyone at Cycling BC was thrilled with this prospect, to have a 23- year-old provincial team coach. There were lots of different egos and characters at the time. It was never my idea to be a BC provincial coach, on top of this I had very thick skin, so all the naysayers didn't really faze me. First year of coaching in BC was not so good as everything was still old school. They had some ideas from some English and Danish training, for example, train on flat roads but not too hard.

I started training with a group of kids between ages 16-20. It was easy to coach them as they didn't know much about cycling and were open to anything. I had to make myself believe I could do it. There were a lot of differences in logistics in the sport between Poland and Canada.

When I won my first race at age 15 in Poland, I was given a new bike, new clothing, paid travel, and a coach. The kids that did not win races, but signed up for clubs, would get older equipment and clothes, but still something. My club in Poland was totally professional, the seniors got a salary and then their older stuff was given to younger kids—sort of like hand-me-downs. The main sponsor of my Polish club was the bus and army vehicle maker, Moto Jelcz. The factory had 10,000 workers. The factory owned hotels all over Poland which the workers would use for vacations, and we'd use for our training camps. It was a good system. Every year the club recruited new kids aged 13-14 and the club provided all necessities to become pro. Kids did not need to be wealthy. Every year the club started with 20 kids. With time, the training got harder and harder and people eventually quit, and only the strongest would continue. Only the best and hardest-working riders would go onto the next level. In my case, only my friend and I made it to the level where we received a salary. We could eat in the factory restaurant for free, and had a mechanic and masseuse on a daily basis.

My background in cycling was quite solid. Since Poland had multiple World Champions in the seventies, I raced with some of the best and had a chance to train with cyclists like Richard

Szurkowski. Poland had some of the best coaching at that time in the world and I got to train with those same methods. So I was able to use my own cycling experience as a professional in Poland to coach these young cyclists. It was a big departure from the way cyclists had been coached in B.C. previously.

That winter in B.C. I began organizing training sessions. I always believed that you won races in the summer with good winter training. My group would do hilly tough rides Saturdays and Sundays. In the old days, most coaches would not recommend hard riding in the winter, just long steady rides. But I made my young riders do tough workouts, they'd ride the Simon Fraser Climb, which is two kilometers long, six times. We'd also use the steep climb at the University of B.C. to practice sprinting all out up a little but very tough hill.

Back at our apartment building job in the East End, the owner eventually found out about our young ages but as she herself was an immigrant from the former Yugoslavia, she was okay with us staying. She still only paid us minimum wages but at least she understood Polish being from the same Slavic language family. She had no problem with my wife attending Capilano College, in fact, she encouraged it. Plus, I had plenty of time to attend to the building. I had lots of time to fix apartment door knobs, clean the underground parking garage and tend to the garden.

One of my very first assignments was to evict a woman who occupied a bachelor suite in one corner of the basement. She was on welfare, so the rent payments were never an issue. But we never saw her, and then there was a strange smell coming from her apartment. According to the law, I could not legally enter her apartment without her permission. But of course my curiosity made me break the law. When she went shopping, I unlocked her door with my master key. My god, I had never seen anything like it, her carpet was soaked with cat urine and reeked, cat food was scattered everywhere, and there were over 15 cats scrambling around! I returned later with an eviction notice. She had broken numerous regulations, and she clearly knew it, as she had no reaction, she just moved out. But still, there remained the problem of the disgusting mess and smell. The owner offered me $200 to clean it all up and prepare for the next tenant. What could I say? Money was money. I took the cash, which was a lot at the time for me. It was beyond disgusting. To start cleaning I had to cut the carpet into smaller pieces and take it piece by piece to the metal bin outside. There was no other way around it. It took me a few days to throw it all out, then paint two coats and install a new fridge and stove. Then, a new carpet was installed. It took a long time to get rid of that smell. It was a real low point, cleaning up that disgusting mess, and I would be embarrassed to tell people I was doing such an awful job. Thinking about it now, we should never be ashamed of what we do for a living and sometimes to survive.

The owners of the apartment buildings wanted us to be more flexible with accepting new tenants. They just wanted more tenants and less empty apartments. Normally we had to do a background check. That was the process; background check, look at their employment status, their past rental references. My wife was under pressure to rent to anyone, so the owners would always have a full vacancy and make maximum profit. So that meant taking chances and renting to people who couldn't provide her with the required information.

Of course, problems started to develop slowly. There was one tenant from the east coast of Quebec. He was very nice and charming when he signed the agreement. Two months later, he stopped paying his rent. He was very knowledgeable about the eviction process which could potentially help him and his girlfriend stay for another six months. He was a pimp and became very disrespectful towards my wife and me. One day he became very verbally-abusive when my wife knocked on his door and asked for his rent. When he was out, I went to his apartment, threw out all his belongings off the balcony and changed the locks. When he got back he became irate. He threatened my wife and called her names. I had no choice but to grab him by his Adam's apple. I learned a lot about fighting from my brother-in-law. He would later become responsible for the unit guarding top Polish politicians including the President of Poland. The pimp never returned and that is what I expected. After that episode, my wife became more selective with new tenants.

However, it didn't stop the occasional confrontations. I had a knife pulled on me and acid thrown on my car by tenants who owed money but did not want to pay their rent. Local prostitutes really liked the building as it had underground parking and it was very large and had no gates. The lights were on all day. I had to get rid of all the hookers, who almost every day left a mess of condoms. I had to find a solution. I made a decision to charge for underground parking. I started checking the underground parking unit at midnight with my camera and with a baseball bat, making their customers pay me $50.

This helped to deter crime as no one wants their photo taken with a hooker and their car window smashed. After four weeks the problem was almost solved, they stopped using the property for their business.

Five months into my coaching with the B.C. Provincial Team, my program looked better and better. I started to see more and more people joining the program. I had a solid group of future racers. B.C. Cycling signed me up for the first high performance coaching seminar for all coaches for all sports at Harrison Hot Springs. It was a well organized three day event with many speakers who were experts in their fields. Some spoke about the newest trends in sports nutrition, others on training, and recovery. It was very inspiring to listen to such highly accomplished coaches and experts. The seminar opened my eyes and made me realize how serious and important coaching was in general and that the only way to be successful was through hard work and a lot of passion. Most professional coaches that were successful were passionate and great speakers. The main and final speaker of the event was Jack Donahue, the famous basketball coach who I'd never heard of before. His presentation was the most inspiring and uplifting. One thing I learned from him that really stuck with me was that coaching was not just a job, it was an art form. For every team he coached, and every player he helped, he was creating a new painting that could not be reproduced.

This was so very true in cycling where the coach could not use the same training program for everyone; every potential racer was a different canvas. At the time I was a volunteer-coach. I started to spend more time with the athletes, and I was completely hooked. The riders and their parents were very supportive and made me realize I was doing something right: becoming a successful leader and making decisions that could change people's lives.

My wife was doing well at Capilano College, which was just one stepping stone in her life to get all the necessary credentials to begin university. She was working hard and her efforts were rewarded with becoming the top student at her college. We were splitting the time to look after our son Peter, who was just starting riding his tricycle. I found a bike for him the first week I worked at the apartment building. I took it out of the garbage container and fixed it up. We still were not making much money but we had flexible jobs that allowed us to do other things and work on our future careers.

My wife set her goal very high: she wanted to become a doctor. I was doing my best at all the jobs I had with the hope that one day it would pay off and a door would open for me.

Poverty was the best motivation for us. We had no family to help us and we were often reminded of where we stood financially in Canadian society. One of the best examples of that was when we decided to buy a car. I found one that I really liked, a Mazda 626, four or five years old. We did not have enough money to pay for it outright, so naturally we went to the bank with full confidence of borrowing $3000 that we needed to close the deal.

We didn't expect any problems with the bank as we had jobs and were not on welfare. After filling out the application, we waited for our file to be processed. Without hesitation, maybe 30 seconds, the banker told us we were not qualified to borrow that much money. It was very disappointing that the bank rejected us so quickly, basically we were too poor for the bank to work with us. We ended up getting car financing from the dealership and we had to pay monthly. That meant that we had to pay a lot more money in our monthly payments. It made us realize again that we were at the bottom of the Canadian financial ladder and that the only way up was hard work and hope for new opportunities.

By the end of 1986, my work as a coach started showing promising results, nationally and internationally. We had good results at the Canadian Summer Games and at the Tour of Abitibi we fielded a six-man team competing against 25 other teams, with half of them being from Europe. My rider, Nathael Sagard, finished second against the current Junior World Champion, Michael Zanoli of Holland. All of my riders finished top 20 out of 150. The first reality check and big disappointment was that none of them were chosen to be on the National Team for the World Championships. The decision was clearly driven by jealousy by the people who were making decisions about the national team selection. Not to mention, most of the people on the committee had never really raced themselves.

My wife started giving me a hard time with spending so much time with the riders and lack of money. I was a third year volunteer who was refining his coaching career and getting good at it. But it was all for fun and not the money.

Coaches in other sports like swimming or track and field made lots of money with results similar to mine.

Riders started coming to B.C. from other provinces to be coached by me. Once, a parent from Manitoba was in town, visiting his son. He approached me, and without hesitation, asked me what it would take for me to move to Manitoba. I was also coaching The Rocky Mountain Team, sponsored by Loomis, and one of the best teams in the country. Most of that was also done for very little to no money. In reality, there were no cycling coaches getting paid full-time in Canada apart from those who worked for the National Team. After some thinking, I told him I'd needed a $30,000 budget for the program and two vans, as well as a full- time salary. The parent who asked me this question was a man by the name of Jim O'Brien. I didn't know at the time, but he was the president of the Manitoba Cycling Association. After I gave him my answer I forgot about it, until I got a call later that Fall in 1986. He reminded me of our conversation in the Spring, and said he had pulled together everything I had asked for, the full-time salary, the $30,000 budget to run the team and the vans.

8

It took me a while to process it all and imagine leaving beautiful Vancouver and moving to Winnipeg which was known for its bitter winters. My wife didn't believe we could do it. I started buying winter clothes at The Hudson Bay, a large Canadian department store, that carried good quality clothing made for very cold winters.

It was time for a big change. The apartment job in the east end still paid very little and was stressful. The owners still insisted on having no vacancies which sometimes caused problems and conflicts. Once a tenant pulled a knife on me after he lost his job and went crazy. He lost it when I went to collect his rent. Good thing I was very athletic and physical from my days of soccer. By the time the police arrived, he no longer had the knife and he was the one who was being roughed up. The police hauled him away and he never came back.

The next thing I knew, I was driving our Mazda to Winnipeg and beginning my "eastern migration" to become one of the first full-time provincial team cycling coaches in Canada. My wife liked that I had a full time job, and started to like me again. I drove through the Rockies and thankfully my very nice London Fog parka kept me warm through the mountains and when I arrived in Winnipeg.

I will say, leaving Vancouver after five years was not without regrets. Vancouver is the most beautiful city in Canada and I had coached there for three years, making some long-lasting friendships and impacting the lives of many young cyclists. For many immigrants and Canadians in general, there is no other choice but to go where there are jobs. You must take care of your family so survival comes first. On my final night in Vancouver, the riders (the adult ones!) that I coached took me to dinner and a boozy night at a strip club, so I would never forget them.

Looking back, when I think about how I started coaching I still can't believe it. I had no coaching papers or car, but we got organized quickly. Parents drove their kids and me to the races, and we'd follow the riders in training with support cars. I set up training rides that are still being used by Vancouver coaches. In three years of coaching there I had seven national champions, future Olympians, among them, Brian Walton, Nathael Sagard and Scott Goguen. Some of these riders are still considered some of the greatest riders in Canadian history and are part of the Cycling Hall of Fame. I am so proud of being involved in their careers.

Canadian cycling started to really grow in the late 80s as a result of the success of Canadian Steve Bauer and the American Greg Lemond. Their successes in the classics and Tour de France made cycling much more popular in North America, since the Tour was now on TV every year here. Riders would come from other countries to race in Canada as there were lots of races with lots of money. Every category had a huge turnout, and it was very competitive.

When I arrived in Winnipeg, I spent the first two weeks at Jim's house with his family. Soon I found my own place, a nice apartment right next to the Canadian Mint. My wife and Peter took the train and arrived one month later. The apartment was really nice, with a wood fireplace and brand new furniture, everything we needed to start the next chapter of our lives. My wife liked the place as it was new and not far from the University of Manitoba.

Here's a funny story about how little I knew about Canadian history. On one of the first days in Manitoba, I was driving around one of the buildings and saw a neon sign which read, big letters: LOUIS RIEL. Given my lack of knowledge of the story of Canada, the name didn't really register anything to me. I just figured it was the name of someone rich. I later discovered he was a Canadian politician and leader of the Metis (half indigenous half European) people. He was hanged by the Canadian Government in 1885 for leading the Northwest Rebellion in Manitoba. A controversial figure, Riel has recently been hailed a hero of Metis rights.

The first part of my plan was to meet all the riders at my new Manitoba office. Basically, it was to see who was interested in my new program. It was the first time in my life I had an office and a desk and I was only 26 years old; it was a big change.

I was not exactly an office person. In Vancouver my office was the roads and parks. But in Winnipeg and -20 Celsius in the winter every day, I didn't have much choice. Only 20 riders signed up for interviews from all categories, junior to veterans. All that was left was to start the serious training. One good thing about it was I did not need to select anyone, whoever showed up was invited. But I still developed a selection system so no one would ever create problems. The first rider to show up at my new office introduced himself, his name was Louis Riel, and only one year older than me, and the most experienced of the local racers. I thought at first he was the rich owner of the building that I had seen many times driving to work. I asked him if he was the owner of the hotel. He laughed and told me about his great, great grandfather. I learned the story of the other Louis Riel, the one that got killed by the Canadian government a long time ago. We became good friends, trained together, and his family invited us for Christmas dinner. Louis was an experienced track rider, and that is all he wanted to do since he managed one of the bike stores. He was the first man to introduce me to one of the best places to ride a bike: Tucson, Arizona. There were no computers in those days so finding out where was the best place to ride a bike in the winter time came from speaking with other cyclists.

This was also the first time I had ever coached women. As a provincial Manitoba coach I was paid to coach anyone with a license. Back in Poland, women's racing didn't exist when I raced. One day back in Vancouver, the owner of Rocky Mountain asked me to motor-pace a girl, as he had no time. It was a lousy day, cold and cloudy, but we went anyway. He lent me his scooter from the shop and after a short introduction, off we went. Not only was it my first training session with a woman, it was my first session motor-pacing as a coach! Unfortunately, after an hour we got caught in the pouring rain. When I got off the scooter I felt very bad for the girl, who was soaking wet and caked with mud, just like me. The first thing I said to her in my broken English, was something along the lines of "cycling is too hard for women, you don't want to do this." I told her she should stick to cooking. Well, I got a lesson that day, because she was far from impressed with my advice. There was a very brief pause, and then she looked me in the eyes, and told me to fuck right off. My old-fashioned views changed very quickly. When Jacob and the boys heard later that I told the Canadian champion that cycling was too hard for women they could not stop laughing.

The first female racer to show up to meet me at the Manitoba office was Cathy Zeglinski. She was a medical student and was only 5'2". I was briefed on her beforehand and was told she was small and not too powerful, that she didn't have much talent and that she would never be great on the bike. Don't bother with her, they said. We had a good meeting. She was prepared to do whatever it took to be a better racer. As a new coach I wanted commitment to the program I was about to start. Despite her difficult schedule at medical school, she started showing up for some hard training in the winter. She would multi-task, and read her text books as she rode an indoor trainer.

My first encounter with the Manitoba Racing Board was to solve a problem with a senior rider who had done something illegal. He'd smuggled drugs in the down tubes of his bike across the American border, just before I arrived in Winnipeg. Some of the board members wanted to go to the police to report what he had done. I happened to like the rider in question. I saw cycling as a path to salvation for this troubled young man. I believed I could get him back on track, avoid jail and have a better life. He had a big heart when it came to cycling, he never let me down. He was a top level competitor. All was forgotten when he started getting great results for Manitoba. It was a good thing that I had managed to calm the members of the board down and convince them to give him a chance.

In Manitoba, it was much easier to organize things than in Vancouver. Winnipeg was a smaller town to get around for training, and everyone lived within 30 minutes at the most. In the first two weeks I met all the riders individually and was able to learn about their goals and what potential talent they had. My next step was to develop a program for each individual so we could survive the long cold winters and remain competitive with the rest of Canada.

As soon as I could, I met with people from the University of Manitoba and got access to their lab and testing facility so I could figure out everyone's individual fitness, their talent and set training plans. In 1987, I was very lucky, the first indoor magnetic turbo trainer had come on the market. It meant an athlete could now ride indoors with resistance. It became the tool that will have a big impact on my riders results and development for years to come and saved my program. From now on we could ride indoors all winter with different resistances and simulate training from outside. Before, there were only rollers with one resistance level.

I bought myself a magnetic turbo trainer and I made everyone buy one as well. It was a game changer, now I could develop a training program to push them to the top of their games.

My coaching experience in Vancouver paid off as many of my riders became the best in the country, I knew exactly what it took to get to that level. A few disadvantages that Manitoba had in comparison to Vancouver was the weather and there were no hills on the top of that Manitoba didn't have as much a choice of athletes. Basically if you owned a bike you made the provincial team, but that was about to change.

It is a big advantage to know what it takes to get to the desired level. Most coaches lack that part of the very important experience. That is why I always encourage new coaches to start coaching by developing lower categories first and slowly with better results and with time automatically progress to work with better riders. That's the way I did it and it helped me a lot. There were so many times that I had seen coaches give advice and training plans to athletes when they simply weren't ready to coached the top talent. Through the years a lot of talent got wasted that way. And sometimes the opposite could happen, an athlete who was not ready for an advanced program risked either getting injured or simply quitting cycling from over-training.

To make my program more exciting I implemented training camps in the winter time to break up winter riding and motivate everyone to do all the training to prepare for the big hills we were planning to ride during camps. First camp was planned for the winter break, right after Christmas for 14 days in Tucson Arizona; the second camp was for seniors for a month and the third one for juniors in South Dakota during March break. In the winter, the whole group would meet five times a week to ride indoors. One of my innovations back then was to elevate the magnetic trainer, to simulate the gradient of the hill. The front wheel would be tilted by a 4x4 piece of wood so it would feel like riding uphill. The rider was forced to use the biggest gear to grind away. All of the training was based on each individual's heart rate range. That's why testing at the university was helpful because everyone had a different maximum heart rate.

My life in Winnipeg was starting to look better and better. Eva was accepted to the University of Manitoba and we didn't have to borrow money for tuition. My son began kindergarten and started riding a bike with training wheels, and later a two-wheeler. Soon, he was playing soccer with other kids on the local team.

But life is never without difficulties, especially for immigrants. After the first day of school, my wife came home in a panic. She told me that she did not understand most of the things her professors were saying. It was one thing finishing her English classes at Capilano college but taking science classes at the university level was incredibly difficult in a newly learned language. We had a big conversation and at the end of it, we agreed there were no options, all she could do was stick with it and try to study even harder. And this is what she did.

She would read day and night. I would be going to sleep and she would be with the book in bed studying. I would wake up and she would be reading and memorizing the same book. It seems four years would be a long road to the finish. Sometimes I didn't think she would make it, but with time she got used to everything and school became a bit easier. She could have taken the easy road and with little education or experience, accepted a low paying job. Yet she chose to strive for something better. Becoming a pharmacist was her goal and she pursued it with all her energy. Good thing our lives were flexible enough that we could take turns taking care of Peter; we didn't need to pay a babysitter.

We always trained together, the Manitoba team. It was the main key for success, in my view. Previously, all the best riders had their own training with their local clubs, but it was not the same as the best athletes in the province pushing each other on a daily basis in the wintertime. I rented the basement of the local hockey arena four times a week, then we moved to the University of Manitoba track and field arena so we could do longer training sessions on the new trainers. Time would go much faster as we watched rhythmic gymnastics or track and field athletes training on the infield through the day. Six hours would fly by. We'd watch the athletes do cartwheels and flips on the mats, or all the action on the infield. There was no problem with motivation. My athletes knew we had to train hard to prepare for upcoming training camps in the mountains and be ready to ride from the first day. With the new magnetic resistance trainers, we could simulate the long one hour hills rides during four to six hour sessions.

Part of my contract included having a big van for cyclists who could not afford to fly and therefore drove to training camps and races. The first one I got was a ten-year-old cargo van, the biggest one available. It was not in the best shape but was fine for our purposes, although it didn't have air conditioning. First thing the Manitoba Cycling Association did was convert it to a propane engine, something new and unfamiliar to me. The propane was supposed to be better and cleaner to operate as well as cheaper. The riders and I built up the entire van with wooden benches, and then had our luggage hidden under a big bed on which we slept or sat. We put all our bikes on the roof rack. The only thing that no one considered was the van had to be filled with propane every 200 km. In the '80s there weren't a lot of places to fill up the tank especially Arizona or New Mexico.

The plan for our first camp was to drive to our destination and switch drivers every four hours. So then it would only take a day to get there, and give us 13 days training. The very first camp we had was in Florida, we were headed to Tallahassee on a very long drive for this camp. We did not have the best start. We had to stop twice on the side of the road to wait for a campground and then a gas station that had propane to open. It cost us two days of training. The second van that used regular gas broke down in Kansas. So the new van had to be driven from Winnipeg and rescue them. On the way back from Florida, the trailer I was towing with the bikes on it got a flat tire. I realized something was wrong after seeing sparks coming from rims in my mirror. I was forced to put the bikes on the roof of the van and leave the trailer on the side of the road. Like I said, this was not an ideal start for Team Manitoba's training camps.

Our next training camp was in Arizona and we made improvements. We added a second propane tank to increase range. It allowed us to travel longer distances between fill ups. We still waited for campgrounds with propane to open on two occasions since the range of the van was only 400km, not enough for the southern desert. We finally arrived in Tucson at midnight. I had no accommodation planned, and of course the internet did not exist back then so my plan was to check local papers from a corner store and try to find something once we arrived. We were desperate for somewhere to stay, but happy we made it to this very exotic place after leaving -30 Celsius Winnipeg. At the local 7/11 store we asked about cheap accommodations since we knew nothing about Tucson. Luckily, there was a man in the checkout line who heard our conversation with the cashier and offered his house. We were exhausted and took the offer without much hesitation. We spent two days at the house of the stranger who I later found out was a university professor. Two days later we found accommodations on Alvernon Street, near the University of Arizona campus, fully furnished. The big bonus was when one of the riders discovered the pay phone by the pool that was broken so we could call anywhere in the world for free. For two weeks we had free calls.

In 1987, I had my first close call as a coach, when my senior team and I were coming back from a big international five days stage race in Niagara. Oneof my riders, Dave Hamilton, ended up in the top ten in the General Classification which was impressive for an unknown racer from Manitoba to accomplish as there were many national and pro teams there. Dave made a decisive break away on the hardest day of the race. Afterwards, I got a compliment from Andrew Hansen, the former national champion who had been on the Loomis Rocky Mountain team in Vancouver two years before with me. He said, "Mirek, what do you feed the boys in Manitoba?!" I knew he was impressed and this made me happy as my little group from Winnipeg was riding strong.

Of course, life is always full of surprises, so on the way back to Winnipeg, I sure got one. I was the only driver for the 24 hour drive the boys were all tired from the racing, and slept in the back. After ten hours, in the middle of the night in the middle of a forest in North part of Ontario I heard a clicking noise. I stopped the van, started checking around the noise was coming from the front wheels under me. I removed the hubcap of the wheel, and there were two bolts undone, rattling inside under the wheel cover! If the wheel had fallen off it would have been catastrophic. I used a wrench in the middle of the night and tightened them up. We made it safely to Winnipeg and the boys never knew how close we had come to a disaster. That was not the only incident with the old team van, and some years later, we were not so lucky.

9

Soon riders from other provinces began coming to Manitoba to be part of my program. This was very unusual considering Manitoba's flat terrain, freezing winters, and very hot summers. It would not be a first choice normally for cyclists looking to become great bike riders. Later in my coaching career I would suggest sarcastically during my coaching seminars to the new younger coaches to start coach in Manitoba if they want to prove themselves.

Nationals were held in New Brunswick one year and those who did well were to be selected for the National team. During the junior road race, a young rider from Alberta broke away for 100 km. He was caught by the group with only four kilometers to go before the finish line and ended up in the ditch from exhaustion. He impressed me so much that I went to the national team coach and said this rider was the star of the day despite not finishing. I made an official call about a rider whom I had never met and declared he would become a champion one day. It was a sad day for him because he didn't make the national team. Cycling can either break you or make you stronger. One of my senior riders, Blair Saunders, spoke to the young athlete afterwards and told him how impressed I was with his ride. His name was Colin Davidson he was only 17 years old. He ended up moving in the Fall from Edmonton to Winnipeg to be part of my program.

My program offered the same deal to everyone, free accommodation and transportation to all our races and camps. The athletes were responsible for their own food. If someone did not want to drive they had to pay for their own airfare ticket. For me as a coach, the first year was the most important to get things going and to establish a solid program that brought results.

In that part of Canada we could only race for four months of the year, in the summer. Local stores would sponsor riders and through hard work and sticking together, we started to dominate Canadian cycling on the velodrome as a provincial team. I knew we would eventually dominate racing despite lacking a large selection of races and not having many athletes riding bikes. There were a small number of races in Manitoba, so it was a difficult time to make it or break it for me as a coach and leader.

One thing that was very important at the time was to make training hard and to make everyone believe that they each would improve and be more successful if we all stuck together. Despite a very small budget of $30,000, the results started to show. Tony Ward made the National Team for track, Perry Scaletta made it to the World Championships on the track and Blair Saunders and Dave Hamilton made the national road team and started to race internationally. At the time I was not aware of what other coaches in other provinces were doing with their programs. A good sign that I was doing something special was the fact that racers from other provinces were moving to Manitoba to be coached by me and other provinces started to follow our lead by hiring coaches full time. It meant we were getting ahead.

In 1987, Canada Cycling Association announced the qualifying races for female cyclists to make the national team for the Tour de France Feminine. There were three single races in Whistler, BC and Ontario. Three riders would qualify automatically based on the accumulated points and four more would be chosen by the National Team coach. One of the first athletes to train with me improved tremendously. Medical student Cathy Zeglinski's competitiveness and hard work paid off. She managed to finish in the top three in points and became an automatic choice for the biggest race in the world. This was great accomplishment despite the cycling community's dismissal of her abilities when I first arrived in Manitoba. Shortly thereafter, I got a call from Canada Cycling Association about Cathy and her experience and background. I said she was an unknown racer who had become very serious about her training and started to believe in herself. But that wasn't good enough for them. I was asked if we could exchange races for her, instead of the Tour de France they would offer smaller, less demanding races for Cathy on other National Team projects in the Fall. They said she would likely not finish The Tour.

My emphatic and quick answer was: No way! Absolutely not. I was completely stunned that they even dared to ask me this. What a ridiculous proposal. Cathy had made the difficult selection process fair and square. There was no way I would let her lose this shot at doing the greatest race in the world. It was such a ludicrous suggestion that to this day I still can't believe I was asked to remove her from doing the Tour de France. Especially given the fact that she had trained so hard, been so dedicated, and followed my program. She deserved that spot on the team just like all the other women. A month later she finished the biggest, most grueling race in the middle of the field and as well as managing not to be the last Canadian. My memories of her racing in France and arriving in Paris on the Champs Elysees will last forever and I am so happy she rode there. I was still a very young coach trying to get ahead. It was a great reward for all her hard work and perseverance that was triggered by my new cycling program and training strategy. Later in her life, that same level of commitment and hard work resulted in Cathy becoming a doctor and Master Cycling World Champion. Persistence and belief always pays off.

My second year in Manitoba in 1988, became very promising. I had everybody behind me, the support was overwhelming. The provincial team was still on a small budget so we ran bingo nights to augment our budget. They were an easy way to make money for future projects, the only negative part was all the cigarette smoke we inhaled during the six hour workday. Back then, of course, smoking was permitted indoors. And sure enough, almost everyone did. The room was a thick wall of cigarette smoke that clung to our clothes. Very disgusting and far from ideal for athletes to be breathing in thick plumes of smoke. Thankfully, those fundraisers only happened a few times a year. Of course, the idea of people smoking in an office, bar, or event would be totally unheard of now but back then it was normal.

Tucson was the perfect place to run winter cycling camps. We had a strong group of racers including Garrett Doray, from B.C. and Colin Davidson, from Alberta. Both had moved to Manitoba to be coached by me. Other riders that I used to coach in B.C. like Brian Walton and Scott Goguen would join us as well. We had eight national team riders training together, 16 riders total. We had epic training rides during the day, followed by epic soccer games in the evening. It was training twice a day and it was always fun. Soccer is not only a good activity for your legs but also helps your eyes and coordination. Plus, we always had a blast. Every day, Monday to Friday we rose at 7am for a walk and stretching and to discuss cycling. At 10 am, our training started with a bike ride that lasted four to five hours, and after that we played a one hour game of soccer, which was hard. Everyone was very competitive, and played it like every game was a World Cup game and we were always exhausted after. There was only one training session on Saturdays and Sundays, a very long ride.

At that camp, Brian was the only person riding a 42x17 fixed gear bike. That idea came to me two years before when I took him and a group of B.C. kids to the Velodrome in Seattle, I wanted to introduce them to something new and different as opposed to the hills in Vancouver. Track racing is an Olympic sport and you never knew where you could find a talented rider to excel in that discipline. It required natural ability and speed. The first day Brian Walton looked good and so natural on the velodrome, which stuck in my head for years. It kept coming back to me every time we met. In 1988, it was an Olympic year. I encouraged Brian to spend more time at the velodrome. But since he was on the 7-11 Pro Team, Cycling Canada wanted him on the Time Trial and Road Race teams, since Brian was the strongest man at the time. So track racing had to be put on hold. That year Brian won the National Road Championships the last time as an amateur.

Looking back, I think 1986 to 1996 were the best years in cycling in North America. There were so many great races and riders. It's hard to say whether it was because of Canadian great Steve Bauer and American Greg Lemond winning in Europe, or maybe it was because of the movie Breaking Away, which became an American classic. Or maybe both.

10

A coach needs his or her athletes to get results in order to earn respect and validation of their work. There's only so much you can say without positive outcomes. Like the old saying: "a coach is only as good as his results". Athletes come in all shapes and sizes and coaches must find the best way to mold those individuals or teams into champions by finding the way for each athlete, make them reach their true potential. Coaches bring their own visions and training methods and personalize them to fit each individual. This is why the coaching profession can be very rewarding not only financially, but psychologically. Every coach can have a big impact on athletes and make a big difference in their future. Many athletes gain their self-esteem by participating in sports. I always worked hard and made every project financially sound. I was good at stretching the budget. Quality of training program was more important than luxury of accommodations. Some people did not like it but the most important thing was the outcomes. We produced results. I never tried to be a role model and more likely would not have been a good one.

I was never a big talker but when I did speak, it was usually about something important. I was generally quite convincing and that was what mattered. Maybe it was my eastern bloc accent or my deep voice that uplifted my athletes, but I never had a problem with motivating them. The main thing is that I never lied to them which was essential to establish trust. Some of my athletes did not like my bluntness. Maybe their upbringing was too sheltered; parents always telling them they were the best and what a good job they'd done, no matter what they'd done. They had never faced criticism or experienced failure. Many coaches who wanted to keep their jobs used the same phrases so they would be likable. without telling them what was happening in the real world. I was not this kind of coach. I did not shield them from the truth and I was sometimes brutally honest. I never set out to be this way but it worked well. When I told athletes that first place was out of the question, they believed me and won anyway. Ha.

1989 started very well for my family. We bought a townhouse and a new car. It was not bad after seven years in Canada to own my first house at the age of 27. It was not easy because we were still paying for my wife's university tuition. We moved to St Norbert, south of Winnipeg close to the University of Manitoba. My son started playing soccer for St. Norbert as well as taking swimming lessons.

There were excellent training roads on that side of town. My athletes would ride 20km out and 20km back on a nice flat road to St Adolf, every day. Sometimes even three times a day. The road to St Adolf was used mainly by me for training. It had smooth pavement, so we used it for all kinds of training, intervals, easy riding, and motor-pacing. We chose not to train much at the velodrome as it was too bumpy. Long ago when they were pouring the concrete for the Velodrome, a train came by and shook up the concrete as it set.

Due to our good results over the previous years, I had a much easier job finding sponsors for the Manitoba Provincial Team. I met some great bike builders in Tucson, one of whom was Bob Gilmour, who moved from Canada to Tucson as a child and later opened a bike shop and started to built custom bikes. My idea was to design a special bike that could be used for the time events on the road as well on the track. The bike frame had to be built with track bike specification and with extra welds to accommodate road gear. Since bikes used in the velodrome did not have brakes or gears, I could swap out the derailleur or brakes. It worked well as riders felt comfortable in the different disciplines as they were using the same bike with the same bike position which was a main advantage. This was something new and innovative, I'd never seen anyone else try it in the past. My team had the advantage of not switching bikes between different training sessions. This way riders could get used to one frame with the same geometry and set-up, as opposed to having to have a TTT (Time Trial) bike, a road bike and track bike. You'd simply remove the derailleur and brakes for the track bike, or add different bars for the TTT bike. It was not only advantageous for training and traveling but financially as they didn't each need three bikes. So I was very happy when Bob built me eight beautiful frames and HED wheels company gave as new disc wheels as a sponsorship. We, just a provincial team, started to look like professionals, with sleek Cinelli helmets and newly designed clothing.

The Manitoba team was not the only highest ranking provincial team in Canada but had the best sponsorship. We looked very good and very strong. Every rider was either a national champion or national team member. Manitoba riders started to represent Canada at races like the Tour de Trump, the Peace Race, the World Championships and even the Tour de France.

I had another breakthrough in my coaching career in 1989. I was asked to represent Canada as a coach for juniors at the Pan American Championships in Mexico City. It was truly an experience like no other. At the time Mexico City was the biggest city in the world and I did not know what to expect. My only visit to Mexico was taking kids shopping to Nogales, the town near Tucson, right at the US border. Mexico City had some great history and a lot of museums that the locals made all the visitors aware of it. Built by Aztec 700 years ago and later conquered by Europeans who changed the appearance of the town forever. Situated at 2200 meters above sea level it was not an uneasy place to visit and compete in sporting events. The first major mistake was sending the Canadian team to high altitude three days before the competition began. When we arrived on the first day, the boys were breaking records on an outdoor velodrome. Mexico had two velodromes: one was made of wood 250m and Olympic distance, where Eddy Merckx set the one hour record. The other was an concrete 333m track with its lanes painted with Teflon, which was installed for Francesco Moser's hour record.

The one meter wide Teflon painted on concrete made training very fast, whereas the wood track was rough and slow. It's hard to believe that Merckx did a one hour world record 49.5km/h on a normal basic bike on that track. Maybe conditions were better 20 years earlier on the wooden Velodrome when Merckx did it, but after two days of high altitude training combined with the air pollution made it hard to breathe. The Canadian boys did their best but had zero chance of medals.

Those young Canadian cyclists learned a lot from that trip. Number one was never to leave your jeans in the public locker room when taking shower, as you risk them being stolen by kids from other countries who were taking part in the competition. On the first day all their clothes were stolen in five minutes. I told my juniors right after to forget about it, the athletes who stole them probably needed them more. They were not as fortunate to be from Canada. In the city we met some friendly people who helped us to get around as I was reluctant to drive a car in all the traffic and risk getting lost in the wrong part of town. Mexico City had two sides: the one for tourists with great restaurants, old monuments, beautiful residential neighborhoods, and interesting things to see. Then there was the hidden side of the mega city with poverty, slums and crime. I began to understand why so many Mexicans risk their lives trying to cross the American border by walking over 100km across the desert with very little to eat and drink. It was not for an adventure like me, nor to escape a communist dictatorship like the Cubans; it was simply to escape poverty and to find a better life. There was a stark contrast between the big villas with tennis courts and swimming pools and the dirty children begging in the streets and some of them living in the gutter.

On the first day, we had breakfast at the cafeteria that was in the middle of the 1968 Olympic Village. There was a huge line up for food and when we got closer to the front I saw men cooking eggs using construction shovels, their sweat dripping on the large metal surface. I could not eat anything. I ordered the kids to leave the cafeteria; we went outside of the old Olympic Village to eat in a restaurant. We would eat there for the rest of the trip. At the end of the trip I was joking with some of the local people trying to invite them to Canada and telling them that we need more Mexicans in Canada, we need their food and their restaurants. At that time Canada started to bring some seasonal Mexicans workers to work on the Canadian farms sines not many in Canada wanted to do the job.

This same year I had the first setback in my coaching career. It happened at the velodrome in Edmonton which was hosting the selection races for the Commonwealth Games in New Zealand. Earlier, my team had won the overall Canada Cup in track racing. It was an accumulation of the total points at different velodromes: Montreal, Edmonton, Calgary, and Winnipeg. The Manitoba team was unstoppable. We had the best bikes, and we looked well sponsored and professional. Team members Tony, Perry and Garret made the selection leaving Per out because he was a first year senior. In the final and most important event, the points race, the team was working for Perry, and he won the race before it was over. Tony and Garrett were doing lead-outs and the unthinkable happened, Garrett crashed 20 meters before the finish. It was a terrible crash, and so close to the finish. He went head over handlebars and landed hard on the track. Garrett was one of the riders who had moved from B.C. to Manitoba to be coached by me. In general, his technical skills were not up to par. He was in excellent shape but his bike handling skills needed work. That is why sometimes we coaches need to devote some training to the technical aspects of cycling. Cycling is not just power and speed. It's important to take time to develop riding skills.

As a side note, another competitor whom I coached also lacked technical skills. She was an Olympic athlete who excelled in winter sports and was even the flag bearer for Canada at the winter Olympics. The only reason she connected with me was to get strong as soon as possible and be a contender for the medals in the summer Olympics. Track cycling was going to be her easiest way of achieving her goal and becoming one of the few to win medals in summer and winter Olympics. For Safety reasons, she needed to acquire technical and riding skills before tackling high speeds in the velodrome. After a few weeks training with me, including receiving a very nice Cervelo bike from my friend Radek at a bike shop for very good price, she became more and more impatient. We started to disagree, she didn't want to ride on the grass which was part of my "learn to ride" training. She wanted to skip that. I wanted her to ride 4000 kilometers before starting to ride in the velodrome. Eventually a National Team coach heard about her past accomplishments and her power ability and got a hold of her making her automatically a national team member and training with the elite. She found someone telling her what she wanted to hear. The other coach agreed to take her on, even though I had told her track riding is very dangerous and there were no shortcuts in this sport. It didn't take long before I got an email from her, saying I was right. She had crashed while riding by herself on the velodrome, so her Olympic dream was over for the time being.

Anyway, Garrett's crash was horrific and he was in a coma for several days. It was shocking for me to see first time my rider lying in bed in the hospital.

The rest of the team returned home to Winnipeg. I stayed with Gerrett in Edmonton hoping he'd say something. He would only respond to me by squeezing my hand. Soon his parents arrived from White Rock.

After five days, he woke up from his coma and his parents took him back to B.C. for more recovery. A comeback was out of the question.

He had been a great talent at age 21 he was the top ten in every track and road event he entered at the Canadian National Championships. In the same year we had the Canada Summer Games, the Manitoba Team had won on paper way before we even entered. My boys, Garrett, Per, Colin, and Blake, were all national champions at some point. The Manitoba Team was not the same after Garrett's crash. Two weeks later Per showed up at my house one day wanting to quit the sport.

While he had been out of town competing, his girlfriend had run off with his best friend. He was a smart and very personable boy but was very depressed after all that had happened. My pep talk didn't help; his motivation, commitment and interest were gone practically overnight. I never saw him again.

I had developed a rock star team that took years to build and in such a short time it was gone. The Canadian Summer Games were just around the corner and I was short two riders. All we had left were Blake Moody and Colin Davidson as I had lost two of my best riders, Per and Garrett. It was almost impossible to find two replacement riders in Manitoba who could keep up with the 50 kilometer an hour speeds in the TTT for 70km. I had a newcomer, Mark Pendera, who had one year of cycling under his belt, and Rick who was totally unknown to me. I joked that we had picked Rick up off the street just before competition. Believe it or not, this was just the beginning of our troubles. With these new riders, it was impossible to predict what was going to happen in the race. The drama started after five kilometers of the 70 km four-man team time trial. Rick got dropped by the team and did his best to catch up but the speed was too fast. Manitoba was leading at every time check with only 3 riders, at one point the television crew started to followed the team at 50km/h. At ten kilometers from the finish line we had a 40 second lead over British Columbia. But more bad luck was to follow, a semi-tractor trailer raced by the team and with the cross- wind, forced very young Blake Moody into the pylons where he crashed hard. Soon after, with help of a frantic Colin Davidson and a loaned spare bike Blake was back racing. It was all reported on CBC news, by the way. We finished second to B.C., and only by a few seconds. Afterwards, Blake started to get telegrams from all over the country, because everyone had seen the entire drama on TV; they couldn't believe it. I deeply regret not being there.

I had started having problems with people in the cycling association. We had developed a strong team. There was no selection process because there were not enough riders to select. When I was traveling with riders those in the organization back home wanted to oust me for some reason. There was trouble brewing. The racing board of directors began interfering with my coaching methods in spite of all of my success. I didn't want to change anything as my training plans were working. It was against my principles to give in to their demands.

My wife was attending university at the time and we also had house payments. I needed my job and it was very upsetting to discover that some people were trying to discredit me and benefit themselves after all my success with the Manitoba team. So I called all the riders to let them know about the situation and my imminent departure. It did not take long for parents and riders to write a petition to the sporting governing body that was above Manitoba Cycling and provided the funding. I was not part of the petition as I always tried to stay out of politics. Two weeks later, the President and VP of Manitoba Cycling resigned, and I was reinstated as coach. I was a riders coach and there must have been a good reason that they stood up for me and made me feel like an important part of their lives. This was the best reward a coach could ever receive.

You are what you are. You have to be yourself because otherwise, you can only go so far. Eventually your true personalities come out with time. I know one thing: I would never have been successful if I had not been myself.

11

After the bad luck and losing my top two riders, Per and Garrett, I had to make some changes to the senior team and take some of my road riders for the National Championships at the Montreal Olympic Velodrome. The sad part was this would be the last cycling event to take place in that state-of-the-art facility that was ahead of its time in 1976. One of the reasons the track was removed and the velodrome transformed into tropical gardens was to make money.

It was a nostalgic event. For three days all the riders wore black armbands because it was the last race there. My team was totally lacking the best line up like before but did not disappoint. Out of 12 teams taking part in just a team pursuit we won four out of six gold medals along with many silvers and bronzes. We took home a big trophy for being the best team of the year. Sadly though, not much later the velodrome was demolished. The results summarized the quality of the program. Life goes on. Just another example of nothing lasts forever.

After the track nationals in Montreal, I needed to go to the five day long junior race, the Tour de l'Abitibi, in Val d'Or, Quebec. Mr. Bonning, who was the new President of the Manitoba Cycling Association, drove the riders there. He was supposed to meet me there. They had two cars: a VW Jetta and the team van.

I got a ride from Montreal with a former professional cyclist, Ron Hayman. I remember he rented a Ford Taurus for the 500km drive from Montreal to Val d'Or.

I can honestly say I never experienced such a drive. As soon as we left the city limits and were on open roads, Ron had his foot on the floor. The speedometer said 200km/h. At first I thought he was joking, then I realized he wasn't messing around. He was driving like an F1 driver. After a while, I took my seat belt off, because at that speed I figured we'd die anyway. We arrived at the race location in just three hours, way ahead of schedule. Turns out that wouldn't matter anyway as my junior team didn't show up. The next day I started to worry.

Of course, in those days we had no cellphones, and no way to communicate. Everything had to be organized ahead of time. Finally, late the next evening they showed up. Oh man, what a horrible sight. While driving late at night they ended up in a ditch, rolling the Manitoba Team van over at high speeds with their bikes on the roof. Some of the riders flew through the windows and woke up in the grass. It was shocking to see all the kids traumatized from the accident, arriving in a rental car. One had a broken arm, one had no skin on his back. They all had lots of bruises and scratches. Thank God no one died. The van was totaled but it could have been a far worse tragedy for Canadian cycling.

We had a team meeting and we made a decision to still enter the race. I found a welder to fix some of the broken bike frames. I borrowed some equipment from other teams and we managed at the end to finish the tour as a team. We were very lucky after all to have Blake Moody severely traumatize finish in the top ten of the biggest junior race in North America. The events of the 1989 season were full of drama, but at the same time we had great results. It was at some level the worst year in my career. Some sports are very dangerous, we never think about it when we do it.

It is always after something bad happens that we reflect and after some time we go back to it.

In 1989 I received some very big and surprising news from Europe. One of my riders, Brian Walton called me to say he won the Milk Race. For those who don't know, there are two Milk Races in Europe. One is the Tour of Britain, one is the Tour of Ireland. The latter one is much smaller. I immediately presumed he won the Tour of Ireland and congratulated him. He said, "no! I won the British one!". I couldn't believe it and corrected him, saying he couldn't have won the Tour of Britain, he must mean Tour of Ireland. The Tour of Britain has not just some of the top amateur teams in the world but some very strong professional teams from Europe. I knew Brian was talented, but there's no way he could have won this race. It was a week-long stage race with very tough climbs, and hard racing. It was also a very famous event. I was incredulous. I still didn't believe him and asked him again if he was 100 percent sure. "I won in England!", he said. After finally convincing me, I still couldn't get over it. The news was amazing, I was super happy. As a young coach, I liked the validation for what I was doing. It's one thing to have my guys winning everything at the Canadian Nationals, it was another to be winning in Europe, the mecca of cycling.

There were so many times during my career that I would tell my athletes stories, so much so it almost became a mantra. I always was telling my riders that the riders in Europe were humans just like us and they were beatable. We just needed to work harder. That is why I will never forget a week later when I received a package from Brian which included one of his leader's jerseys from the Milk Race. I was so proud of him.

Some of the athletes I coached on many occasions had no money and could not afford to pay rent. I ended up giving them a place to stay in my home. Cycling was not the most popular sport in Canada at the time and it was hard to find talented cyclists ready to commit to being full-time athletes.

So when such an athlete came along, I didn't want to lose them. Prospective talented riders could be anywhere, I just had to find them and develop them-no matter their financial situation. No other coaches were doing this at the time.

One such border was an athlete named Tara. Tara was a survivor, a warrior. She was a street smart person and was a naturally disciplined hard worker. We got along from the start and for months, had no major problems. When she stayed with me, now and then she'd bring a young man home whom she was dating at the time. She was a young woman, after all. Months went by and then one day, she didn't bring a man home, to my surprise she brought a woman. Two days later, she unexpectedly moved out with the woman and our relationship came to an end. I had never before came a cross of a open lesbian relationship in my coaching at the time so I was in shock. I was a naive immigrant and did not know how to react. Tara left behind a letter for me to read. She told me how hard it was for her to be gay sometimes, but she respected me as a coach and was sad to go and one day our roads may cross again.

Where I came from we never talked about people with different sexual preferences. As a kid we joked about it, but none of us actually knew any gay people or at least people that were out of the closet. There were no open gay people walking around in communist countries as it was dangerous for them. They were forced to hide their sexuality in order to live a peaceful life. Apart from jokes at school, we were forbidden to talk about it. My parents never discussed it, most likely because of the Catholic church. It was part of being a good christian- to demonize homosexuality.

So I came to Canada with this ingrained view and it manifested itself on my first day on Davie Street in Vancouver when I saw gay people. I had never witnessed homosexuals living their lives out in the open. And to be honest, my already ingrained negative opinion got worse before it got better. I would tell gay jokes and my opinions during discussions to my riders on the long 20-30 hour drives to camps. Little did I know back then I had gay athletes in that very van on many occasions and they were very uncomfortable and maybe scared. It took me six years to change and realize how wrong I was and how much my words hurt them. One of the big reasons for me to unlearn some of my thoughts began when Tara moved out and left the letter for me. For months she had tried to tell me despite all the verbal jokes and innuendos she endured. All of our time spent together made me realize we are pretty much the same, we came into this world as equals and she deserved to be respected, no matter her personal choices.

12

It must be the nature of humans to endure, and in 1990, the season was coming fast, and we tried to put the 1989 problems behind us. Things returned to normal. Our new president Mr. Bonning possessed good leadership and team spirit. Over the winter, he organized team parties at his house to make everyone feel comfortable and get to know each other. I had new goals for the 1990 season. The first was to find new riders for the Canada Western Summer Games, it required teams of five men and five women. This for me was the hardest part. In a country that focused on hockey, baseball, football, track and field, and other sports, it was always a big challenge to find athletes who wanted to race bikes in Canada. Remember, it was still a fringe sport back then, especially in Manitoba. So I was always on the hunt for new riders, new talents. Then, I had to not only convince them to try cycling, but to determine what their strengths were and to help mold and transform them into champions.

I started a new program on November 1, with physiological testing at the University of Manitoba. Testing for me always played an important role. It was a shortcut to create an individual training plan. Testing took a lot of the guesswork out of coaching and revealed a cyclist's maximum potential right at the start, rather than waiting the two to four years it otherwise took to determine talent and strengths from the racing results.

On many occasions athletes were training for the wrong events. It was never pleasant alerting a cyclist that they were in fact focusing on the wrong event. This was not something a cyclist wanted to hear. The best example of the importance of changing events for athletes was Tanya Dubnicoff. We discovered Tanya, who had a background in ice hockey, after the Manitoba Cycling Association started advertising for new recruits. Although it was late Fall, we continued to train outdoors as long as the temperature was above -5 Celsius.

She first showed up on a cold and windy day and didn't have gloves or a hat. We were doing laps on the grass in the park trying to avoid riding on the road where windchill could get up to -20C. I sat watching them from my car, and thought I'd never see her again after 40 minutes of freezing temperatures. At the end of training she came to the car to warm up and then biked home. To my surprise, she kept returning. She told me she wanted to be on the Time Trial Team for the Canada Western Games. She was a big and strong girl but in endurance sports that is not always enough. A big engine with a high VO2 (oxygen consumption) is also required. She wasn't quite suited to endurance and I saw her getting dropped in the long intervals all the time. I did know she had power, though. But I had no idea just how much. One day I told her to join me on a ride. I found a little 50 meter long uphill on the Winnipeg Red River flood-way, and challenged her to beat me on five sprints up the hill. To my surprise I could hardly out sprint her. At the time I was winning Category 1 races so I was in very good shape. After training I asked her if she would like to try track racing. Her power was suited for the one kilometer time trial, known as the kilo and 200m sprint.

She was not happy to be taken off the team time trial squad but I reassured her that she would be very suited to this. Next, I found Tanya a track bike, a nice Bianchi that we drove one evening to pick up from the local ex rider for a steal at $400. Finally she was ready to change her focus to the track. In training Tony Ward, a national champion himself, would help her navigate the technical aspect of riding track and her progress was phenomenal. Good results came very quickly, all in the same year. She won medals at the Canada Western Games, as well as the National Championships, which meant she was automatically on the National team. Who knew three years later she would be World Champion in sprint, and eventually a three time Olympian.

It is interesting to note that testing also revealed that Tony Ward was misplaced in his discipline. Tony wanted to race every single event in cycling when I first arrived in Manitoba. But I told him we had to do testing first; without testing, it was like making a kite from unknown materials and hoping it would fly. After testing him it was obvious that he should stick to track racing. With his talent and perseverance, it didn't take long to become a track and team pursuit champion and eventually represent Canada at the World Championships and other big events. This is why I believe testing is essential in finding riders' strengths and potential and matching them with the right event.

That winter, the team started training for the first training camp of 1990 which took place right after Christmas. I never allowed any athletes to come to the camps unfit and unprepared for heavy loads of training. We only had two weeks at the Christmas camp, and we had to maximize our time, averaging four hours of training a day, and riding 40km long hills some days. If they would not get ready and prepared, the risk for injury and getting sick was too high.

I had some new training ideas and decided to use myself to test them out. I always wondered how much extreme heavy weights would help road racing. Everyone new lifting weights for the track was important, but what about the road? I started working out with Tony who was already doing weights four times a week for his specialty 1km TT and sprints. After two months of heavy lifting I went down with the team to Tucson for the Christmas camp. I felt very strong riding the trainer prior to departure, so I felt confident even though I had gained eight kilos from weight training.

I always rode with my athletes during camps. This was my rule. I never ever followed them in the car unless I was motor pacing. I thought it was important for me to do the same training and I really liked biking and occasional racing anyway. On the first three hour ride I got my answer. It was supposed to be a fairly easy leg opener after a 24 hour drive to Arizona. Yet, with the extra weight, I really started to struggle on the small hills on the first day and on one of them I started to pray for flat tire since I did not wanted to get dropped by my riders and funny thing was I got one just before the big hill. In the next two weeks we would often do epic training rides up climbs called Kitt's Peak and Mt.Lemmon. The climbs were approximately 100km away and once we cycled there, we'd all race up to the top. The Kitts Peak mountain was a seven to eight percent grade for the last 20 kilometers, and on one of the days of our one of the epic rides it got quite foggy and cold. On the long ride to Kitts Peak, Mr. Bonning was driving the support car, and another support staff had a camera. At first I felt fine riding up the big finale hill but the last 10 kilometers did me in. By then I was by myself, with no food, feeling cold, totally exhausted and riding in the heavy fog. As the van drove by I waved frantically to get it to stop and pick me up but they didn't see me. Funny as I remember seeing the whole episode on film later. I couldn't turn around as it was too cold to go down the hill. To this day I don't remember how I climbed the last five kilometers or made it to the van. I do remember sitting in its nice warm interior and discovering that the riders had eaten all the food I had prepared for myself. I had bonked and could not recover as I had nothing to eat. It was an epic day to remember or forget.

I struggled throughout the entire camp even though I felt strong off the bike. It took a long time to lose that eight 8 kilograms of muscle that I had gained from heavy weightlifting. I concluded that although my general strength had improved, the extra weight hindered my hill climbing. Climbing is all about weight to power ratio so the lighter you are, the better it is. My strength up the hills never got better; I was much slower. My weight training experiment was over and I never recommended weight training for road riders again.

Back in Winnipeg, the Manitoba Cycling Association was still looking for new recruits who could be eligible for the Canada Western Games. We tried to approach hockey coaches to convince them that cycling would help improve the fitness of their players by riding in the summer. For some reason they did not buy it. Nowadays, hockey players, speed skaters, and soccer players all use cycling for extra fitness. But back then they didn't like the idea. There was always a chance an athlete would not go back to hockey or their other primary sport, they said. I didn't think this was such a bad thing as cycling is a beautiful sport. It was unlike many other sports, it offered opportunities to travel and see the world and enjoy beautiful scenery and to be outdoors.

A woman named Andrea Auch was working in the Manitoba office as an administrator. She was always enthusiastic and made sure everything was running smoothly. After work, her other passion was coaching speed–skating, a sport that was in her blood and in her family. One day Andrea asked me to meet one of her speed skaters whom she thought had great potential to be a cyclist. I was open to meeting new prospects, especially as we needed more cyclists on our team. It was minus 20 degrees Celsius as I watched my first speed skating competition outdoors. After 5min I could not tolerate cold any more and I went inside the clubhouse and waited for the races to be over. Soon after, this smiling, pretty red-headed girl approached me and introduced herself. Her name was Clara Hughes. The most important thing was that she owned a bike. That was step one. Who knew she was to become one of the finest athletes in Canadian sport history.

13

Running a training camp for 20 young riders is a big responsibility. In 1990, we ran a winter camp in Black Hills, South Dakota. We stayed in cabins near Mount Rushmore, where the four presidents faces are carved into the side of the mountain. It was the first time I had an athlete with a nut allergy, so I made it very clear that no one could have any nuts in the cabins at any time. The first day there, we took all the riders shopping to Rapid City. Just two days later, in the middle of the night, one of the young men ran to my cabin to tell me that the rider with the peanut allergy was having trouble breathing and had forgotten his allergy medication in Canada. I hurried him into my car and drove 40km as fast as I could down the mountain to Rapid City where there was a closest hospital. His condition was worsening, his throat and face were swollen and he was having a very hard time breathing. Luckily we made it on time. Later I found out that someone had bought some peanut butter and left it on the knife that was used by the rider having the reaction.

It seems like every year, new problems arose during these camps. I wonder if the parents realized how much organization and hard work went into planning these training sessions and the tremendous responsibility taken on by the coaches on and off the bike. Two weeks of taking care of 20 young athletes was no easy feat. Cycling is a dangerous sport and as a coach you are in charge of the athletes safety, especially when they are riding on busy roads and being passed by large transport trucks.

Near the end of camp, we planned for the cyclists to ride 100 kilometers with the last 20 kilometers mainly uphill. This was to be their longest and most challenging day. Most of them were already tired from all the previous rides so this was to be an epic day. The weather in the morning was 15 Celsius, so we dressed lightly expecting the temperature to remain the same all day. No one even brought a windbreaker. We started the ride the same way as always with 20 kilometers down some hills, but after two hours of riding the sun disappeared and conditions began to worsen. We kept the pace up and some of the girls dropped off and I stayed in the "lead group" with the fast boys. Suddenly the weather became alarming. When we were still about 30 kilometers from the cabins, it started to snow. The girls were smart and waited out the storm in a grocery store far behind us but we kept going up the mountain where we stayed in the cabins. We were in the middle of nowhere surrounded by forests. I put my bike in its biggest chain ring and hammered it to get back to camp to get the van. It was freezing cold outside and only one of the riders had kept up with me.

I grabbed some blankets and started driving through the storm to find the other riders. I could barely see a thing with all the snow falling. The visibility was so bad I could barely see ten meters ahead. I kept driving, looking for my riders. I couldn't see them and was getting worried. I was anxious that something had happened to them. I continued to drive very slow, scanning the road ahead of me. Nothing. Eventually, after about 10 kilometers, I spotted them in a ditch all in a huddle trying to stay warm. What a joyous sight-seeing all of these skinny kids trying not to freeze, I didn't know if I should laugh or cry. I know one thing, if their parents had seen them in that state they would not have been laughing.

The next day we continued on as if nothing had happened and resumed our training. It's as if all the trials and tribulations we endure as athletes and coaches in training are not important, we are judged only by the results. That is all anyone remembers. By the time the Canada Western Games came to town, Manitoba was ready. We won the most medals in all the track events.

Every year, our most important racing event was Nationals. It was very important for us to keep up our winning streak. Other provinces started following our lead and hiring full time coaches. It was a no-brainier that they were falling behind. In 1990, Manitoba again won the most track medals in all categories at Nationals held in Calgary. With only a handful of riders, we won 14 Gold medals in junior and senior categories. At first the competition was so weak it was almost boring to watch all the events but the future will tell that we had exceptionally talented athletes on the Manitoba Team who will be eventually racing for the medals at Olympics and World Championships and other international events in the future.

During this time, cycling was really taking off. Same year one of my riders, Colin Davidson who moved to Winnipeg from Edmonton Alberta won a road race at Canadian Championships as a first Senior Canadian Pro Champion. This time his racing strategy paid off and it was to get out ahead and ride solo for most of the race, just like he did back in junior category when I noticed him for the first time. I saw him try this unsuccessfully as a junior but this time as a Pro rider, it worked. Later, he became a professional, and competed at the 1992 Olympics. He had such talent, he just needed to be polished like a diamond.

My wife and I enjoyed watching television in the evenings. Once a week there was a show featuring a fortune teller who would read a person's future using her cards. It was live so people would phone in, but it was very hard to get through. I did not believe in any of that stuff, but my wife was fascinated by it. At least she must have had some talent as they gave her so much time on television. One evening that October, Eva decided to call in. She got through, I couldn't believe it. I could hear Eva talking to this lady live on television. Eva asked about her future, and the fortune teller read her cards. They showed a future in the medical field and lots of success of course.

At that time my wife was still a student, and did not know 100% what direction to follow. Next, my wife asked the medium about my future. She asked if I worked in sports, to which Eva replied yes. Without a moment's hesitation, she declared I would have six athletes in the Olympics and would win three medals. She had no idea I was coaching cycling, the hardest sport to win multiple medals. Her prediction was comical. I really thought she was nuts and a fake. Her idea was even more preposterous given that the Olympics was only 16 months away and none of my athletes had qualified as my team was so young. No one from Manitoba had ever won a medal at the Olympics, ever. One thing I never took into consideration was that she never said at which Olympics I would get medals. I quickly forgot about the prediction, and I started to think about next year's training program.

14

Almost ten years had passed since I had emigrated from Poland. My situation was better, I could afford a trip home, and most importantly, the chances of being arrested for not returning after my vacation were nil. Communism had ended by then and they would have most likely forgotten about me. The system had changed, but some people had not. During communism there was no such thing as unemployment. Everyone worked who wanted to work. The difference was this time the mentality had to be changed. In the old days there was never competition between companies. And most of the population didn't have to compete to be as productive as possible. When I went back, all I heard from people were complaints about this new way of life. It was obvious that nothing would be perfect overnight. It was the promise of progress, just like in more advanced countries. Lots of smart and young people were coming up who did not know the old system. It would still take some time to get rid of old communist ways, like corruption.

It was a good trip, for two weeks. My old cycling club was doing well, getting financial support from the city and from private sponsors. I went for a bike ride with my old teammates who still raced. It was good, I got to ride every day. Everyday I visited family and friends and ate and drank too much making sure I did not hurt anybody's feelings. I think I gained more than three kilograms during those two weeks.

Ten years is a long time to be away. Everyone was happy to see that I had a house and a good job in Canada which made me feel proud of my accomplishments at the time. Polish people tended to be more judgmental in nature compared to Canadians who did not care how much money others had or what car they drove. Soon after I left Poland, my parents deeded the house we grew up to my sister. She then sold her house and moved in with my parents. My name was taken off the deed. It was nothing new, many of my Polish emigrant friends experienced the same thing and could relate to me. It was just the way it was. When you left very quickly there was nothing to come back to.

The first training camp in 1991 took place like every year, during the Christmas break. We stayed in a great furnished apartment in Tucson. There was a large swimming pool in the middle of the complex and it was all very well maintained. One day we were sitting at the pool relaxing and swimming after a long ride. At some point one of the riders told me I had a phone call. I went back to the room. I picked up the phone and it was Colin Hearth, head of the Ontario Cycling Association. Colin Hearth was known in Canadian cycling for helping Gord Singleton, Steve Bauer and Karen Strong develop from young ages. He was an older gentleman, and I liked his dry sense of British humor. Once during track nationals in Montreal Colin got very animated. It was sort of funny how loud he got with his strong voice. We all were all wearing black armbands to protest the demolition of the velodrome after the end of nationals but Colin was wearing them on his arms, ankles and neck. He looked very funny. Colin was coaching a rider during the last race of the competition, the points race. He shouted every lap for him to move up to the front of the group. The kid never moved up and was riding at the back of the pack, after ten minutes of shouting, I remember him finally screaming loudly "you're going to be good in another life!" and he left. I could not stop laughing.

The last time I had seen Colin was at the Tour de l'Abitibi at the customary last night party when the race finished. Everyone drank too much beer. Every year it was the same. At the discotheque, Colin, the Russian coach, and me were hanging out and one of Collin's riders came up to ask us what we were drinking. I replied that I drink Johnny Walker and the Russian coach chimed in that he liked vodka. The riders were being a bit silly and we couldn't quite figure out what they were up to. Soon, the riders returned and asked us to come outside, which we did. And to our surprise, we saw that they had brought a super- sized bottles of booze, a magnum. I later found out that they had found a tunnel into the warehouse and were stealing bottles. A huge lineup materialized outside the disco as juniors lined up to drink stolen liquor. Needless to say, I was hungover and feeling quite ill the next day when we were driving back to Manitoba. Luckily, our president Mr. Bonning was the designated driver. I did not get drunk like that for another ten years and it was to celebrate a much bigger occasion.

Anyway, during the call back in Tucson, Colin told me how impressed he was with my coaching. How I had won 15 gold medals from a small talent pool the year before. He asked me straightforwardly if I was willing to move to Ontario and how much money it would take to hire me as an Ontario coach. Ontario cycling had had many unsuccessful years despite the largest membership in Canada. Every Ontario race during the racing season had 100-150 riders to compete in Category One and Two and over 100 in junior races, not to mention other categories. So, Colin saw that they needed to hire a full-time coach. They had a huge talent pool and should have been getting better results. Like so many other provinces, Colin knew Ontario had to follow Manitoba's lead and hire a full- time coach. It was the last of the provinces to do so.

15

I was very surprised by the offer in spite of the successes of the Manitoba team under my direction. With only 20 racers, Manitoba had collected 15 gold medals at senior and junior Nationals. In those days before the internet or cell phones, news of my success spread slowly by word of mouth and by looking at the results. Colin told me that I was his number one choice, despite there being a lot of applicants for the job. All I had to do was say yes, fly out for an interview and accept the conditions. There was no need to formally apply. The salary I asked for was not an issue, and I ended up being the highest paid cycling coach in Canada. In April I was flown by the OCA to Toronto for the interview and it went very well. I told them what they wanted to hear, they told me what I would like to hear. Most importantly, I was to have a good budget of $30,000 to take athletes to the camps and races. At the time it was a lot of money, and I needed a big van to take riders to events to insure nobody would miss out on any training set out in the program.

The final part of the puzzle was where I was going to live. My office was to be in Toronto but with the way I coached I knew it would not work from there. I was not a coach who worked from an office, I had to be on the road, on the ground with my athletes, riding together. I told the members of the board how I needed to live where there were hills. Since Ontario did not have any mountains, the closest thing was the Niagara Escarpment. I was a bit familiar with the Niagara and Hamilton region, and I remembered the town of Dundas from years before. My provincial team from British Columbia had won many medals there in 1985 at Nationals. Dundas is a community and town near Hamilton Ontario. It is nicknamed the *Valley Town* because of its topographical location at the bottom of the Niagara Escarpment on the western edge of Lake Ontario. It's a beautiful little place, with lots of hills, and parks. It has a quaint little downtown that has shops and coffee houses, a few nice pubs and restaurants. It's got a small town vibe, but still close enough to the highway, or Hamilton itself. I always liked it.

That request surprisingly didn't create any problems. I could work from home and set up a training center two kilometers from the well-known McMaster University. The OCA was clear with their goals—they wanted medals at Nationals, and Ontario riders to go to the Olympics and World Championships.

In the end they all agreed to a five year vision involving the 1996 Olympics. My new job as a provincial coach was to start after the 1991 Pan Am Games where I was to be the Canada head coach for track and road events. It was not an easy decision to move to Ontario. Manitoba had given me my first full-time position coaching job, and allowed me to make a better life for myself and my family. My wife was very young and very smart. We did not need to borrow money to pay for anything, we had a good set up, and prices were lower in Manitoba. Eva had one more year of university to finish so my son and I would have to spend the first year in Ontario without her.

Coming to Ontario was a big change, It was the biggest cycling association in Canada, with over 2,000 members. The racing calendar was packed with lots of stage races and prize money. It was just missing a coach and structure. The selection system needed to be revamped for the provincial team. Since cycling was very big in Ontario, they created their own little world of cycling. They had their own stars in their province, and favorites. I had a lot of work to do, changing the system, improving the success rate outside of the province of all of the Ontario riders and making them more competitive. Change is always problematic and controversial, especially when the system has been the same for so long. That was my challenge, make changes and try not to anger too many members of the old guard.

But before my move to Ontario, I still had to be the Cycling Canada coach at the Pan Am Games in Cuba. I didn't know much about Cuba, one of the few remaining places where Communism still existed. The only Communist country I had ever been in was my home country of Poland. In general, I figured the situation was the same. A totalitarian government with people fleeing when they could. People who were equally poor, locked inside borders, with robot-type jobs.

When I arrived in Cuba, I could not believe how bad it was. It was very different from Poland. The local people were very friendly and welcoming although they had very little to eat and very few possessions but it was safe to walk around. I never saw any beggars on the streets. The food in restaurants was very basic as well. I remember eating chicken, rice and beans every day.

The Canadian team had to bring their own toilet seats to the Games Athletes' Village. There was no hot water in the shower, but that was not a big deal as it was 35 degrees Celsius outside. There was no air conditioning in the rooms, so we slept in a puddle of sweat every night. In no time, my skin got the darkest I'd ever seen it, and my hair bleached the blondest I had ever had from swimming in the salty water of the ocean. The sun was so strong. It was not at all like Poland, the place where I had left. It was for completely different reasons that Cubans would risk their lives on boats or other means to escape to Florida. I had many conversations with a woman who was cleaning my room every day. She was originally a teacher but became a cleaning woman to earn points for a family vacation in the restricted zones in Varadero resort. On our last day in Cuba, the Cuban government took us by bus to Varadero. It was the total opposite of what I had seen so far in Cuba. An absolute paradise for tourists. Everyone was drinking, eating all-you-can-eat buffets, beautiful young men and women everywhere, looking to make money. Clearly the Cuban government wanted us to spread the news, come back another time and spend our money when we weren't racing.

All the riders were per-selected by Canada Cycling Association. I had originally met the team in Winnipeg ten days before departure. I was in charge of team final preparation. Unfortunately, none of the team members were that strong. Only two were really fit. It was a total fiasco. One day they couldn't even finish my simple training program. In the end, I said forget it, let's go to a bar and have some beers. Five days was not enough time to prepare them. About ten days later, Tanya Dubnicoff won a gold medal in the women sprint. The boys struggled to finish the road events and the TTT. The women were a bit better, but it was disappointing to lose to the Cubans. At least all three of my Manitoba riders that got selected to represent Canada won medals. It was not a personal success for me. The important part was making sure my riders ate only cooked food and drank bottled water. On the last day I gave all my Canada team clothing to the cleaning lady.

My parents and me

Riding my first bike

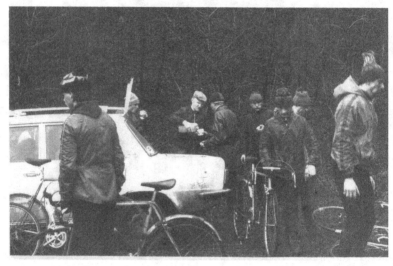

Training with the team in the 70s

Campo Latina

First accommodations in refugee Campo Latina

Aunt Staszka visiting us in Latina

First wedding

Working on Mercato in Rome

The Town of Amelia

Ready for the first job in Canada , cleaning houses

Going shopping

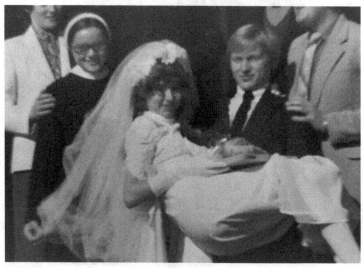

Wedding in Church with Sister Josephine

Wojtek „ Johny", my first athlete

Apartment building Menager job with some help

Group training in Vancouver

BC Provincial junior team. The Dream Team

Eva receiving price for the best student in Capilano College

Traveling to the training camp with Manitoba Team

Manitoba Team winning on the velodrome

Colin Davidson winning the Road Nationals for Manitoba

First time back in Poland

With Canadian Team in Mexico City

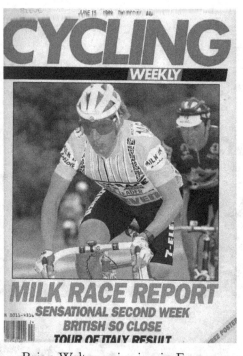

Brian Walton winning in Europe

With Manitoba Team in Tucson Arizona

16

After Cuba I moved to Dundas with my eight year old son Peter. I was going to rent a small apartment but two of my riders in Winnipeg decided to follow me to Ontario, so I arranged for a big townhouse so they could sublet from me. It was a financial risk as the bigger place was expensive to rent. My wife was against it after all the trouble we had with tenants in Vancouver. She knew that we could be stuck with the rent for one year if the riders changed their minds and moved back to Winnipeg. It didn't ease my mind when the parents assured me there would never be a problem paying their rent. My wife was right at the end.

During the first week on the job, I met a lot of people, not just riders and coaches, but race organizers, members of different committees, parents, bike store owners. As I expected, not everyone liked me. Some were afraid of change to the existing system. Some didn't like that young guy, 30 years old, was calling the shots.

One of the first things I did was to develop a new selection system that no one could argue about. It was simple, based on results only. To make the provincial team a rider had to produce results in different races, so there was no politics involved. Before my system, Ontario had a coach's committee that would select different riders for projects at their monthly meetings, which in my view was a not very fair and waste of time. With my system, a rider could have his own coach and his own program and if he produced specific results he was an automatic into any provincial team projects. Strangely, some people did not like not to be part of the selection process. There were hundreds of riders in Ontario and for the limited budget, I could not accommodate other coaches' opinions. Since my way of selecting and putting over 40 riders from all categories on the provincial team based only on results was a better way and being friends with the coach was not enough. After the selection system was introduced, I created a program for the year for all who made it. The goal was to make Ontario number one in Canada since it was the biggest province.

Some riders that made the provincial team strangely did not want to take the opportunity to train with the best at the training camps. They followed their parents and their own coaches and their own program. No one could accuse me of selecting only the riders I coached or Iliked. I started testing everyone at McMaster and I was lucky to meet the best in the field: well known professor Dr. Duncan McDougall and Dr. Bogdan Wilk, a professor from Poland who helped me a lot with the access to the university facilities and their experience in testing.

My goal was to not let any talent slip through my fingers, Ontario had a big population and a lot of talent. In the past that talent would flourish on its own but it took a lot of time. Many riders didn't make it because they were not tested, lacked direction and never trained properly. In one year there was no one left from the old members of the provincial team. The new faces on the provincial team were a result of a new program, testing and hard training.

One of the biggest surprises for me coming to Ontario was to find out that my cousin Ted immigrated to Canada as well. Ted was much older than me (16 years) and he decided to leave

Poland at age 40. He had a good job as a teacher in Poland and occasionally when I was a kid he would take me to his school to play soccer with students he was teaching. My first trip to another country was with my mom and Ted. We went to Italy to visit my aunt when I was only 12. It is an amazing coincidence that out of my many cousins, Ted was the one who shared with me the first impression of the capitalistic world in 1972. Then, 20 years later our lives connected across the ocean in Hamilton. His immigration path was not much different than mine.

Like many immigrant stories, he worked shift jobs, picking strawberries or working at car cleaning places. That was okay until he had to do that in the winter. Ted never really complained. He also volunteered in Hamilton as a teacher with children with special needs. Eventually he was rewarded for his volunteer work just as I did and promoted to a full-time paid job there. This made him very happy. From my point of view, I could not believe that someone like him with a high education and a great job in Poland, someone who had seen so much of the world, was cleaning cars at his age. So I was glad that he got the job he was meant to do and he was naturally born for it.

After years of not seeing each other Ted couldn't believe I was all grown up, married and with a child. The last time he saw me was when I was 16 years old. He was so happy and proud of us. He started watching my son Peter at basketball and we became very close again, just like in the old days. After a year on her own my wife finished her university classes in Winnipeg and moved to Dundas to join Peter and me.

It took no time to sell our first house, and all the furniture inside of it. We lost a bit of money selling it so fast but we needed the money to start the new chapter in Ontario. It didn't take Eva long to find a pharmacist job in Hamilton. After ten years, we finally settled in, and accomplished our dreams.

Some people end up doing this faster, and others take longer. For us, it could not be done any faster. We were a young couple with a child without any family here to help us. Work made us move three times across the country and it was a normal learning process for any immigrant to go through. We came to the new country without any knowledge of the new system. When I look at those first years, I look back at them with pride. All the experiences we went through helped us understand others in their journey. Many older immigrants left a good life and better established lives for hope that the new country would provide something better. They found out after a few years it was a mistake and there was no way to go back.

After my wife got a well paid pharmaceutical job, we started to look for a house in Dundas. It was the first time the two of us had well paying jobs at the same time. Luck was on our side, the economy was bad, it was a recession. Housing prices were very low but it was still a challenge to find a house in our price range. I didn't want a huge piece of land, just a half-acre and not too far from town. Location was important to me. After four weeks of driving around, we were heading down some small streets just outside of Dundas, and I saw a "For Sale" sign for a small house without a garage. The house was made out of brick, maybe 50 years old. What caught my eye was the property. Half an acre with mature trees and lots of room for improvements. I stopped the car and it took me ten seconds to figure it was too nice and out of our budget. A man came out of the house and waved to us. I drove up into the large driveway and he invited us in. My wife did not want to go inside; she didn't like the look of the house--it was too old. After a little persuading, she agreed to go inside. The owner was a professor at McMaster who was recently widowed. He had a new girlfriend and wanted to move in with her and her children. So, he wanted to sell the house quickly. The price was $185,000, but he said we could have it for $145,000.

For us that was a lot of money, but thanks to the recession we ended up paying less than the land was worth. My wife was giving me a hard time as she wanted to live in a newer house.

This house needed a lot of work. To begin with, it needed new windows and a new bathroom. So for the next two months I did all the repairs we could manage financially. It was nothing special but it was much better than the pink toilets and old bathtubs that I replaced. We also installed new windows and the kitchen was modernized. For the three of us it was a perfect size; plus with the large property with a large driveway we could build anything in the future.

I loved the area, too. Dundas Valley Park had mountain bike trails and hiking trails. The Bruce Trail was one kilometer away. There were big waterfalls close by that we could visit every day during long walks. The main cycling attraction was the famous Sydenham Climb and it would prove to be very important to my training program. It was the number one reason I chose to live in Dundas.

As all the years before, we started training on November 1. Our next winter camp was set to take place in two months at high altitude in Pine Valley, California. In February and March we did our final touch ups and trained very hard just before the season. It was very important that my riders were contenders from the first races they entered. As I always would say, you win races in the winter training. To me the winter preparation was crucial for consistency in the summer. As the senior camp took place in California, I organized camp for the juniors for two weeks in South Carolina during their spring break. I would fly there to make sure everything was done my way. The young riders were properly hardened up since cycling is the hardest sport in the world, and athletes need to be ready to be able to train three times a day if the program required.

In June and July, we spent two months in Allentown, Pennsylvania for track training and road racing. Unfortunately I did not have much time to see my son winning basketball or cross-country running since I was always away. One day he came home at the age 14 with a big basketball trophy. They had gone to London in Ontario and won a street basketball tournament against these amazing kids from Detroit. Peter was a natural at basketball. He would make 24/25 free throws in competition. He always amazed me with his focus and precision when it came to basketball. What was amazing to me was that he was also not only superb in endurance sports, but had such superior hand-eye coordination. It's not often you see cyclists or runners who can also play basketball so well. I was so proud of my son. But I wish I had been there to see it.

17

ore and more riders started coming to Ontario to take part in my program. It made me feel like I was doing something right, like I was making a difference in other people's lives. I was so busy and preoccupied with the entire program. Yet, every rider could make me happy if they worked hard and with time the expected progress and results would come.

One day I got a surprise call from ex-rider Brian Walton. At the time the only rider more known in Canada than Brian was Steve Bauer. Brian had signed with the top professional team, Motorola, which was the new sponsor of the 7-11 team. We never really lost touch, but we hadn't been talking as much as when I was coaching him.

In the early '90s the average speed of the pro peloton had increased by four or five km/h. New illegal super drugs hit the pro racing circuit. When EPO made its way into the bike racing world, many young pros died without doctor supervision. Their blood got so thick it was like molasses and they would die in their sleep. The worst part about cycling on many occasions was that athletes that used drugs in their career were back in sport after they retired pushing them to younger upcoming prospects and that is one of the reasons it was hard to find clean winners in cycling. Brian couldn't keep up with the stress and demands of the new high speeds of the peloton, and started to fall ill from fatigue. Same with Bauer, a guy who used to be in the yellow jersey in Tour De France and one of the top pros. Brian's contract was not renewed.

Brian called me and asked me to coach him again, like the old days. My first reaction was that he should be coaching me. He was the one who had such great results in the top level of cycling. He had an impressive career, he raced with some of the best, had done the Tour of Italy, Paris-Roubaix, and more. 30 years later I asked Brian why he called me that day for help with coaching. His answer was very simple, he said he worked with many people in the past and I was the only one who couldn't talk him out of doing training. I was the only coach who made him do the training program and believe in it. He was too smart to think that he could achieve anything by himself without a coach.

From my point of view, chemistry and understanding play an important role in both sport and normal life. It's hard to get any success in life without support from. The first time I met Brian as a kid at 19, I didn't like him. For a couple months he was asking too many questions and acting like a know-it-all. But that changed as he grew older. His return to my program was like a "missing link". He was a good addition to my Ontario team program with his Euro experience and the big races under his belt. As a coach I tried to be a strong leader but I needed a rider to play the role of a captain who would help execute the hardest moments of the training plan.

In my opinion, every successful venture needs strong leaders to keep up morale and encourage the team to work hard to achieve set goals. In 1993, my program started to prove that it deserved to be defined as a high performance program. Ontario riders started to place top ten, at the World Championships, international competitions and dominated the Canadian scene.

With Brian, my vision of a high performance team was possible. It was back in Seattle when I first coached him that I noticed his natural talent on the track. That picture never left my head. 7 years later to his surprise, I told him we would have to find a track bike and start training seriously on the velodrome. At the time Brian had a new cycling contract with a North American number one professional team and his team manager was very supportive of this idea. Tom Schuler, the owner of the Saturn Team, loved my idea of Brian racing track at the Olympics. My biggest headache was coordinating his training and track racing with his personal team road racing program. The team got him a track bike right away. But I think sometimes they thought my idea was a bit crazy, even Brian was initially skeptical.

We had a rocky start, right from the beginning in 1993. In the fall of 1992, Brian had contracted mononucleosis, so his winter training started to suffer. For a very long time, he was lying in bed with no energy to move. The first ride he did was 20 kilometers, almost at his maximum heart rate. As a coach I never had experienced that kind of virus. All I could do was think positively, despite deep fears inside me that my best rider would never recover all of his strength. Since Brian lived in Vancouver we could only talk on the phone. When things slowly improved, the rides became longer and faster. The only good thing was that he had gotten sick in the off season so that when January came around Brian was ready for the new training program.

18

The 1994 season came very quickly. Not much had changed with my high performance program. There was a new event for the UCI World Championships: the individual time trial. It was good news for a coach like me since I had many good and strong time trialists in my program. Plus I had been a pretty good time trialist in my own cycling career and through the years I always put a lot of emphasis on my riders being strong at it and to try to win races solo. My personal experience was paying off, my athletes were making the national team. We ended up in the top ten five times at the World Championships in road events.

In 1994, Anne was second and another rider from my program was fifth. But it was also marked by some bad news. I learned one of my ex-riders was taking drugs. After she left me, she started to get help from bad characters believing she would get faster by cheating the system. It was discouraging to think that an athlete who had come up through my program would turn to performance enhancing drugs, but she was the only one. Over 400 athletes took part in my program throughout my career and not one person could ever say that I encouraged them to take drugs to ride faster.

In 1995 the Olympic qualifiers began. No longer was it the case that cyclists would go to the Olympics based on coach's choice, and not all countries were assured of entry. Cycling was getting big, and a selection system was necessary to ensure that only the best would be able to participate. Nations needed to earn points to qualify. Athletes had over a year to earn points to gain a spot for their country. For my athletes we had one early season event in Argentina which was the Pan American Games, then later in the year we could qualify in the World Championships in Colombia. Compared to European countries, we were at a real disadvantage. The one qualifying race was at very high altitude and the other one was too early in the season to get 100% ready. We did not have the 8000f altitude to get ready for the Columbia. After much thinking I decided that it was best to prepare Brian for the Pan Am Games early in the year rather than wait for the other qualifier later in the Fall. It seemed a better way to get him to the Olympics rather than risking waiting until later in the year and racing at altitude. You could never predict what would happen.

The plan was to spend eight weeks at a training camp close to San Diego, in a town called Alpine. We were near the velodrome so we could train on the track as well as ride in the nearby hills. Brian came to the camp well prepared with a very solid training base. I would use those two months to get him totally prepared for the Pan Ams. The plan was to enter three races in Argentina, the individual pursuit, the road race and the points race. The training plan was hard, but what made it harder was my new innovation, what riders called "the death machine."

It was an old Swedish bike trainer, a Monark, that I bought from the YMCA for 100$. It was hard to believe that the YMCA would throw these machines out. With the help of frame builder Mike Barry, we cut the back out and welded dropouts where you could attach a regular bike. There was nothing electronic on it; everything was adjusted manually. The speed, the tension, everything was done by hand at first. Riders attached their racing bikes and could do intervals and I could measure watts and RPM. It was the first of its kind in Canada, to me it was another tool to improve and be ahead of the game. Compared to indoor trainers now, it may seem primitive, but it helped many of my riders become champions at the world class level.

EPO (blood doping) was everywhere in 1994. The speed in races picked up three to four km/h. So we had to be smarter if we wanted to succeed cleanly. Being aerodynamic on the bike was important and we finally got access for Brian to be tested at the University of Indiana. Their big turbines were normally used to test the aerodynamics of planes so Brian looked out of place. Paul Lue, the master of producing aerodynamic equipment, helped us arrange it all. I drove to Indianapolis for the tests.The plan was that the engineers at the university would do their best to work on Brian's position in the wind, then I would give my thoughts. It took many hours, but they finally found a position where Brian's body sliced through the wind. The only person who was skeptical was me. It was one thing to look "aero" but the question was, could Brian still put out at least 400 watts for ten minutes in that optimum position?

Sure enough, the ``death machine'' proved that the position was not optimal. He could only hold 400 watts for a minute. The position looked fast, but there is always a compromise between aerodynamics and power output. So, with three weeks to go before the Pan Ams, we adjusted his position again. Finally he could hold over 400 watts for four minutes. Without the help of the death machine, there was no way you could properly test bike position. It was obvious that aerodynamics is one thing and comfort is something else at top speed. The final step was to bring speed to Brian's legs. The track in Argentina had a very fast concrete surface but it was outside and often very windy. Brian's legs still felt sluggish, it was hard to do proper speed-work in Alpine, maybe it was all the mountains and no flat roads to ride. I made a decision which, looking back, was a bit crazy. Since Brian was not showing any progress with his speed and there was nowhere to motor-pace where we were because it was too hilly, I had a new idea.

One morning, I told Brian to put his bike in the car and told him that we were going for motor-pacing. He was surprised as it was raining that day, so he had figured we would be taking the day off. But it wasn't raining in Yuma, it was nice and sunny. I told him we were going to Yuma, Arizona, in the desert. It was the only flat road around. We drove for 1h over the mountains to get to the desert on Highway 8 and we stopped on the same Highway. Brian got the bike out. There weren't too many cars on Interstate I-8, just some trucks now and then. He got behind the car and I started slowly driving at 60km/h. I gradually went faster, and faster. After 10 minutes I was driving at 100km/h. I judged the speed and the effort by looking at Brian's face through the back window of the car since I knew him very well. We even passed some of the trucks! It was kind of scary. But at the time we just went for it.

We kept up the pace and when we passed a jail in the middle of the desert, the police noticed us. Imagine seeing a station wagon driving along at 100km/h, and a scrawny cyclist a few centimeters from the bumper, pedaling 140 rpm in his 53x11 gear. It was quite the sight. It was super-hot that day and the police just pulled up beside me as I drove along, I smiled and waved. They looked at their speedometer and then me again and just shook their heads and drove away. It was very funny at the time, and we were lucky there was no one on the highway. We were driving above the minimum speed limit so we weren't really impeding traffic for 100km nonstop, but looking back it was quite dangerous. We stopped just before Yuma. Brian's heart rate had been close to maximum the whole time. When we put his bike in the car, I felt his tires, they were very hot and ready to explode. But that single session transformed his legs. It took his speed up to another level. It was exactly what he need it.

A week later, the Pan-Am Games began. First up was the track competition. Brian entered the four km individual pursuit. It didn't go so well but he still won the bronze. Only the top two would qualify for the Olympics. After his first race, I was nervous about the remaining races. Since I wasn't at the Games, I was not sure why he had not performed better and up to his ability. A week later, I found out when I saw a photo of him doing the pursuit on the cover of Pedal Magazine. He was clearly back to the position that the engineers created, without my modifications. So, he could not produce the same power output. Next up was the points race. It's a good thing he used a different track bike, it was the same set-up as his road bike. It was no contest; he lapped the field four times, and got the first Canadian ticket to the Olympics. The road race was another victory for Brian. Despite the Americans having their top professionals George Hincapie, Freddy Rodriguez and Bobby Julich, Brian managed to come in solo, and thereby qualify Canada a full men's team to the Atlanta Olympic Games. A year later Brian would have his road race slot removed. But by that time we were used to that sort of thing happening in Canada, we had been dealing with the same people through the years. A year before, in 1994, I received a letter from the Canadian Cycling Association. It informed me that I was not welcome to be around my riders at the Road World Championships in Sicily who were contenders for the medals. I went to Sicily with Brian only for track events and we got two top ten results. After I flew to my family in the north of Italy. It was obvious that someone there wanted to take credit for my years of work. But overall, 1995 was a good year for my program. We earned medals at the World Championships, the juniors won the National Championships, and my senior team pursuit also won the National Championships and were unbeatable again.

For years, we were dominating the Canadian scene, and I had several riders who were contenders for the Olympics.

19

That Fall I started to renovate my house for the second time. I used to help my dad a lot with his renovation projects and had worked in construction in Italy with the great masters of masonry. I learned a lot and now I could apply it to my own house.

I worked on the new kitchen and the bathroom. I bought two marble mosaics, made in Italy, to install on the floor. The bathroom was all marble, it looked nice. I did it on a limited budget but with time it doubled the value of my house. Since I did all the work I didn't need to borrow money for it, since the labor was free. My wife found a job at the biggest pharmacy chain in Canada. Finally, all her hard work and perseverance paid off. We got a "new" used car to save money. A nice one-year-old VW Passat. We were working harder than ever. I was on the road over 180 days of the year.

Peter was 14 years old and was also busy. He was doing cross-country running, basketball, and sometimes on Sundays if he found a ride, he would do a bike race. He was hard-working and made me very proud. He started getting very good at free throw tournaments, winning them all at the time. His running success took off as well. It was good to see my son had a strong drive and didn't have to wait for me or my wife to find something interesting for him to do. He was getting involved in everything he wanted to do by himself just the way I was when I was a kid. I was totally in my cycling and Olympic mindset and my son was putting his best effort to be the best in whatever he could set his mind to. Life was not getting easier because we were all working harder. There was no time to think about it or reflect or analyze our life, we were just on the run.

It was 1996, and my 12 year coaching anniversary was coming up. I was finally at the top. With the Olympics on the horizon, I knew I had finally made it. Everything had worked out; my dreams had gone from fantasy to reality. My athletes slowly started to become contenders on the international stage. Pressure to succeed was growing and I began to experience sleep problems. I put a lot of pressure on myself which led to very painful migraines, which were sometimes so strong, they made me vomit. The headaches got so bad I sometimes had to go to the emergency room at the local hospital. For the past four years I had been working 180 days of the year, away from home. I wasn't the kind of coach that sat at home, enjoying a meal with my family by the fireplace, coaching over the phone. I was always on the road, with my athletes, working hard and try to get better.

Things got heated with the lead-up to the Olympics. Canadian Cycling Association chose the coaches for the Olympics and told me I would not be given coaching accreditation at the Atlanta Games. They said it was because I only had the first two levels of coaching certification which was a great excuse for the media. The chosen Olympic coaches had no riders in the Olympics but they had great coaching papers which they had a lot of time to work on. I had many riders who were contenders for medals, but it was obvious that someone there wanted to take credit for my years of working with the same athletes that came out of my program. But who cared? It was just a piece of paper. Surely I had proved I knew how to coach at the top level, with so many of my riders going to the Games. My athletes took a stand and organized a petition with threats of boycott. They took it to the media, and they even took it to the races and post-race interviews leading up to Atlanta. Soon, the press was contacting me and it was stressful and unpleasant. As an immigrant with a strong accent and my blunt approach, I was never good at playing games or politics with people who had government jobs. I never liked interviews. But it was very satisfying to see my athletes acknowledge my work publicly and stand up for their coach like never before.

Later that year, we had the Olympic road trials in Saint Sauveur, Quebec. All my riders were very well prepared for the upcoming race. The race would decide who was going to represent Canada at the Atlanta Olympics. It was actually a very difficult road race, up and down a very tough hill, dozens of times. My gut was telling me that something bad was unfolding and a new controversy would hit the media. I knew Canadian Cycling Association would have some kind of excuse for why one of my riders couldn't go.

Brian's top performance at the Pan Am Games had automatically qualified the whole Canadian team and he spouse to be automatically selected. At least that is what they told him at the time. Soon after the Olympic Trials race, not only me but everyone else received a shocking news, Brian would no longer be racing the road race at the Olympics. Now there were two stories in the media about me, the first that I was not invited, and second, Brian the top Canadian racer would not be doing the road race. It was just hard to believe, especially after all my riders dominated the qualifying races, where so few finished. There was more controversy after the women's race where one of my riders won solo and after the race she spoke out about the whole situation on the medal presentation on the stage in front of hundreds of people. She said she had won the race for me. She went on to tell the media she would boycott the Olympics if I didn't go. The next day it was all over the papers. Even Steve Bauer said it was a bad unfair decision made by Canadian Cycling Association to exclude Brian from the team.

The men race had been long and very technical, with only a handful finishing. Bauer, who was the most accomplished cyclist in Canada and my son's hero, won the race. All Ontario athletes did very well as well. When everything was over, two of five riders to make the cut were from my team as well two of three on the women's road team. The only one still not qualified was Brian. He did qualify for track racing along with another athlete I used to coach in Manitoba. So, there were a total of six out of 11 Canadian Olympic riders who had come from my program. It was a shame that Brian got shafted from the road race. But thanks to the petition and threats of boycott from my riders, I ended up getting a coaching pass to the Olympics from Cycling Canada. My athletes showed that they could not only race hard, but they could fight hard for the right causes. They spoke their minds and were blunt just like me. I was very proud of them and their appreciation for my years of work and my dedication.

After the trials were over and it was clear who was selected, my next big job was to figure out the last big training phase so they would be in the best shape possible leading up to the 1996 Olympics. In April, Brian injured his knee cycling in Europe and it was taking a while to heal. It took some time to rehabilitate and he ended up eventually having knee surgery as a last resort. With only eight weeks of training left, I knew the importance of a positive attitude and having confidence in the program that everything would be okay.

I knew that our winter preparation laid a great base and that an athlete could come back if they'd done their homework over the winter. My program was focused mainly on endurance strength, the base for everything else. There was still hope that Brian would regain his top medal contender shape for the track event.

Brian and I went to Allentown, Pennsylvania with my Ontario team. He started training hard three times a day, one hour on the rollers, two hours on the track, then evening road rides for two-three hours. It was very hot in Allentown, that is why we would stay and train until the Olympics. It was an important decision.

20

My aim was to keep my riders away from the heat as much as possible during training. The Americans with their big budget had their national team camp in Atlanta in brutal heat to acclimatize the athletes. Their coach's approach was different from mine. He believed that riding lots of slow hours in hot and humid conditions was the best way to win medals. In contrast, I had my athletes ride at the coolest time in the day and mostly high speed training. Those weeks of hard training flew by. My decision and approach paid off. My athletes were showing freshness and positivism at the end of the long camp.

Since we spent a lot of time alongside the US national team during training camps in Alpine and Allentown over the years, I always tried to measure myself against their program with their money. They had top coaches, doctors, mechanics and a 5 million dollars budget. They couldn't believe we stayed in Alpine and slept on air mattresses we'd bought from Walmart. Meanwhile, the US team stayed at a hotel with air conditioning and an all-you-can-eat buffet.

After being accepted as a coach for the Olympics, I finally received my official coaching pass that allowed me to be at the start line with my riders. It was a badge of honor that my athletes fought for a long time with the petition and threat of boycott. What a change it was from the letter I had received in 1994 before the World Championships in Sicily prohibiting me from being around my riders.

I drove to Atlanta with a car I borrowed from Brian. Everybody else flew, but it was all worth it. Three days into the Olympics, Canada won its first medal and it was in cycling and a rider from my program. It was Canada's first ever medal in road cycling as well if we don't count the 1984 Olympics with its communist countries block boycott. We were all over the newspapers and Canadian television.

The next seven days were very nerve-wracking. Brian's points race was coming up with 28 of the top class racers from 28 countries. The race was 50km with 20 sprints and the last sprint was double points which would be the game breaker for Brian and me. The points race involves a mass start and a sprint is held every ten laps on the 250m velodrome until the end of the race. Points are awarded to the top finishers in each sprint. In training, Brian kept posting faster intervals every day. His injury was totally gone and he started showing more speed with more freshness. I'll never forget, as Brian made his way to the start line with me, we were both joking, trying to pretend we were calm, but I saw his heart rate monitor and his heart rate was 120bpm, he was nervous and anxious and so was I. I was holding Brian on the start line pretending it's all okay, it's not a big deal with thousands of people watching in the stands and on live television. It ended up being a very fast race from the start. Brian was in the top-ten in points after the first half of the race, and it started to rain a little. I started to do a rain dance, as I knew if it rained heavily, they'd stop the race early and Brian would finish top ten. Top ten at the Olympics would be very impressive for Canadian. Little did I know, there was a much better result on the horizon.

The clouds came in and we had a couple drops of rain but not enough to stop the race. Since Brian was not a sprinter our game was always to break away and lap the field. In the points race, lapping the field was worth 20 points compared to winning a sprint (1 to 5 points) so if the rider laps the field he doesn't need as many sprint points. In the second part of the race, Brian found a moment to counter-attack after a sprint and got a 100m lead on the 250 m track. It was very close. It took a few seconds for the other competitors to react and start chasing. Brian was out there with two other riders and the group was closing fast. I was on the infield feeling my heart in my throat. For me, the whole race seemed to be taking place in slow motion. A group was closing in, they were 20m behind with one lap to go. Brian outraced them all and received double points on the final sprint with an unbelievable effort. He got second after all the points got counted. Canadian famous cyclist and track sprinter Curt Harnett told the press afterwards that Brian was like Superman. He had never seen anything like it. Brian's comment after the race summed it all up. He said he was not the strongest out there but worked the hardest. To me, it was a miracle after all we went through in the last four years. My consistency and stubbornness had paid off. I was only 35 years and after 12 years of work and development I had three Olympic medals on the road and track and four top-ten places. Sue Palmer did not disappoint, racing remarkably in support of her teammates and finishing top- ten in the road race.

Remember that crazy psychic from television six years earlier? Well, she was right. At the time, I had only envisioned the Olympics two years out (Barcelona) It never occurred to me that she meant six years later (Atlanta).

21

Once the Olympics were over, I drove back home with my wife and Peter to Dundas. I was totally exhausted mentally and physically. For the last four weeks I had been taking pills to fall asleep and then a lot of coffee to wake up. The only good thing about it was I could artificially sleep but taking any pills is not a good idea in the long run. I was lucky my wife and my son drove to Atlanta to not only share this amazing experience but to support me through my exhaustion. It got so bad that I struggled to stay awake at the CBC studio for television interviews. After all the stress and hard work, I wanted to go home. I gave some short interviews and then hopped in the car for the drive back to Canada. I was elated and tired and it was time to take a rest and get rid of my unhealthy lifestyle.

This was not easy. Sponsors were calling, riders were calling, journalists were calling. The mayor of Hamilton sent me an invitation and next thing I knew I was part of a parade in Hamilton for local Olympians. It was a new experience, I'd never been driven around in a luxury convertible through city streets with people waving everywhere. It was a big deal and it felt good. People were finally interested in what I did for a living.

The next big acknowledgment was from the Prime Minister of Canada. I was asked to fly to Ottawa for dinner and a big celebration. All Olympians who had earned medals and their coaches were invited. I was still tired and exhausted but I would never pass up the opportunity of going to Ottawa to meet the Canadian Prime Minister, Jean Chretien. It was a great trip, we had a magnificent dinner and got a private tour of Parliament. I sat in Chretien's official office chair and had a chance to shake his hand while he thanked us all for our contributions. I flew home very happy with many great memories and experiences that would last a lifetime. Looking back, I definitely would do it again if I had to. Life is all about experiences that we create for ourselves. Sometimes they are bad, sometimes good. I always try to remember only the good things that made me happy then and still do when I remember them now.

My happiness didn't last very long at home after the Olympics. Soon After I received a letter from the Ontario Cycling Association. I was laid off, I had lost my job due to the tough economy. The new Ontario government came to power and made cuts to the budget. One of them was sports. My mind felt hard from the very top of the pedestal and felt hard. I started to have nightmares and anxiety attacks, I would wake up with numb arms and legs which was terrifying to me. It wasn't because of the layoff, it was all the pressure I had felt for a long time before the Olympics. The worst thing was the panic attacks I started experiencing on a daily basis. They felt like electricity going through my body. I ended up going to the hospital and getting tested, but there was nothing wrong physically with me. I debated looking for a new job since coaching with my resume would make it easy to find a position. But with my conditions it was impossible. I had to stop thinking about cycling completely. I stopped answering phone calls from riders. I stopped meeting people. I visited many doctors, did many different tests, with not much success. I had always been strong mentally, a leader. I had been healthy, riding my bike every day with my athletes keeping them mentally strong. I was full of confidence. Now, I was lying in bed or on the couch, feeling sick, unemployed, scared to go outside or pick up the phone. Since panic attacks cannot be controlled, I never knew when they would happen I gained weight, I had no energy to do anything, I felt bad. After a couple months I decided it was time to do something about it. I started with 30 minutes on the bike. It did not feel great but it was a good first step. It was very hard at the beginning to force myself, but I did it. I was pedaling for survival. I decided to try something different from coaching since I was in the wrong head-space. I planned to work on my house and increase my property value. The plan was to rebuild my house and to build two additions including a four-car garage and four more rooms. My wife thought I was going crazy when she saw me drawing plans on the kitchen table for my project. She did not think it would ever happen. She saw the drawings and plans I was preparing to take to the city for the permits. It was not easy, at that time there were no computers to get the quick information on how to do it so I relied on what I had learned in college in Poland. I had done something similar in school, but the difference was instead of drawing simple houses made of wood I was drawing plans that employed large machines and tools.

To start with, I familiarized myself with Canadian building codes and standards. I told myself that it must be an easy thing to build a house from wood. I just needed to follow construction guidelines. My drawings got approved by the city engineers, and I got the permit with only some small changes to my project. I counted exactly the amount of materials I needed so it would be pre -cut and make a building addition much easier and faster to build. A week later my wife came home from work and could not believe what had happened. There was a big backhoe excavating the new foundation around the house. Mud was everywhere. Now she knew I was serious.

At first, I got two construction companies to quote me a price for the project, but despite the poor economy, they were both out of my price range. They wanted $140,000 and I could only afford

$60,000. The renovations were quite straightforward and simple. If I wanted, I could do it myself. Being totally preoccupied with the construction and a lot of work that came with it improved my mental health. I was so busy working fanatically all day long that I stopped thinking about my problems. I still got the occasional anxiety attack when I worked too hard but overall was feeling much better.

During my son's spring break, I felt well enough to travel to California to ride in the mountains again. We stayed at Sue's Palmer apartment which she was renting out while she prepared for the new racing season. When I got back, I had lost a lot of weight. I decided to hire two construction workers to help with the project. I found two older Italian men who had worked in construction all their lives but were out of work in the recession. I paid them by the hour which helped me save money. My anxiety attacks became less frequent and one year later they were gone.

I had taken a long break from cycling. My construction was almost finished and in the summer, I started up a new private coaching business with clients from Canada and the USA. I managed to stay in touch with old athletes as much as I could. It was sometimes new and undiscovered territory for me, charging cyclists money for coaching. In 1997, I was the first Canadian coach to offer coaching services over the internet. Mazurcoaching.com

22

Since computers were the new thing at the time, I did not believe that Internet advertising would work. I got one of the racers to design my first website and buy advertising in cycling sites and magazines. I was very skeptical about people paying for coaching. But my Olympic success paid off. I got more riders hiring me through word of mouth, rather than advertising. It wasn't like now with Facebook ads and all that.

Soon I was making more money than when I was a provincial coach. My customers were from Canada, the US, Europe, and Japan. They represented all fitness categories from beginner to world champion. It was a big change for me. For years the best riders were selected, and the objective was winning. Now I was selected by the riders. Their objective was to be a better athlete and the progress was geared to individual improvement. I had riders who were preparing for world champs, but I also had riders who just wanted to get stronger and one day possibly race their first race.

At the end of 1997, I really started to enjoy coaching again. I was riding my bike with the athletes I was coaching and I started to enter local races. I offered a similar program that I used as a provincial coach which included running three training camps. Some of the riders I coached were from far away so cycling with them at the camps was a way of getting to know them from a coaching point of view. We went to South Carolina in the early winter, then San Diego in February and March. I also offered private camps for very rich customers.

After a year of renovations, I was back at what I do best: coaching. My program started showing signs of success by my athletes winning three national championships in three different countries: the USA, Poland and Canada. It was unheard of in coaching to win three national championship jerseys from three different countries and later on in my private coaching career they turned to three national professional champions from three different countries.

Toward the end of 1997, I had my last project organized: camp in Boulder, Colorado. It was a high-altitude training camp in the big mountains. On one of the rest days I took a walk through downtown Boulder. On the main drag I bumped into pro cyclist Julie Young. Julie had lost her job with the best pro team in the US and months before she asked me to train her to get back to the top. We walked the streets of Boulder, where all the hippies and vagabonds hung out. People sold all kinds of kitschy stuff in these funky little stores. In one of the stores that sold homeopathic items, there was a sign for fortune tellers. In the past I didn't believe in this stuff but then I remembered the last encounter on Winnipeg TV that predicted my Olympic success. It took some time for Julie to convince me to go in for a reading. But I figured, why not as she was paying. It could be fun. The fortune teller was an older, Indian woman who was composed and professional despite all of my joking around. She sat with me at a small table and put her hand on my head for about 20 seconds. She said I had a strong aura around me and it was very easy to read me. That made me pay a bit more attention as I didn't know what she would say. Next she described my leadership style of how people trusted me with what I do, and how I am an old soul. I said sure, with some sarcasm. She remained serious and then she said that in the early months of next year I would get a big job offer, a big opportunity of a lifetime but I should really think before accepting it because I could only be successful at anything if I followed my heart and did it my way. I was never comfortable working for someone else or following orders so she did make sense. I should always follow my intuition because that's where my success comes from. I kept joking around the whole time. There was no way someone would offer me a job without me applying for it. There were not a lot of opportunities in cycling after the Olympic year. Julie went in after me for a reading, we had fun analyzing it all and I forgot quickly all about it.

23

The next year in February, at the San Diego camp, I was walking with my riders on the sidewalk, walking back from dinner in a small town called Alpine. A car pulled up beside me and I saw a familiar face in the window. It was one of the members of the United States Cycling Federation. He had met me many times at competitions over the years and we did not need an introduction. He asked me first what I was doing in California and then he told me about an opening for a full-time US national coach. This caught me by surprise. After some conversation I got his card and he drove me to the Olympic Training Center. It was a huge center near San Diego for all sports, not just cycling.

Two hours later I was offered a dream job, to coach the US national team. This was my fourth coaching job offer, and like the others, I was approached and offered the job. I never had to apply or show a resume. It was all fantastic and a great feeling knowing that other people respected my work.

Soon I was flown to Colorado Springs to visit the USA Cycling Training Center; it was the head location for all American national teams, for all sports. I had signed a four-year contract and received an advance payment to help move my family to Colorado Springs. It seemed everything was great from every point of view, but next time I flew to Colorado the second I got out of the plane and took my first steps in Colorado, I felt weirdly uncomfortable about it all. Right off the start my instincts were telling me this is not the place for me.

In general, I am not accommodating to others and never was. I liked to stick with my instincts and beliefs and not be swayed by others. I was not the guy who could be bought when it came to sport. However, I started the job and got used to the way things worked in the US. Almost immediately, I discovered that one of my top rated juniors was using and bringing recreational drugs to the athletes dorms. He had talent but my decision was simple, he had to leave the program. The problem was that he was from a rich family and the people above me thought he deserved a second chance. My tough decision was not popular and I made enemies within the cycling association. Soon after, I noticed my job was changing. Instead of working with the athletes on a day to day basis, I was more and more sitting at a desk booking tickets and do other administrative tasks. At the time I was still waiting for my work visa to travel freely to and from Canada. After four months I was so tired of everything that when I got stopped and interrogated by the US border patrol, they asked me why I traveled so often, and since my answer was not good enough, I was told I could not enter the US anymore. My response was "thank you very much!" I grabbed my bags and left the airport. For the first time I was happy I could not travel to the US. That didn't last long as my work visa finally came through. I lasted another four months before deciding to pull the plug. This job was not for me. That ended my job as the head coach for USA Cycling. Lucky for me, I got a good part of my contract paid and went back to private coaching.

I believe that things happen for a reason in life, and that good or bad will lead to something bigger and better in the future. All I had to do was return to basics and be myself. I would never go to a fortune teller again since I was too easy of a read. It was a time to work for myself again and do what I was meant to do, helping people that would come into my life for coaching.

My son Peter had started bike racing before they had official categories for him. When he was nine years old, I would sometimes watch him through the window draw a finish line on the pavement and make all the kids race around the townhouses in Dundas. He rode a small BMX bike and the funny part was he would let all kids go 20m ahead before he started the race.

By the age of 14 he started to take part in local Hamilton time trials showing impressive speed. I already knew he was talented. The first time I noticed he had the ability for endurance sports was when he was 12 years old and part of a study at McMaster University researching fitness in kids, and use of Gatorade. He was happy to do it as he got paid with a coupon from the hospital for Nike Air Jordans. Part of the study was to test the VO2 of every subject. After his first test, the numbers were so impressive that I ordered another test since I did not believe they could be right. Another good sign of talent was Peter's ability to win cross country races. A soon as I was finished with my adventure with the US national team, I started helping my son to become a better athlete. We drove to big races in the US and Quebec, just like the provincial team in the past. Just Peter his friends and me. It was becoming very clear that Peter was showing great potential and he really enjoyed biking. In Canadian cycling history Canada never had a World Champion in the road events, riders that I coached in the past came very close on a few occasions but it never happened.

When Peter was 16 it was time to call Canadian Cycling Association to find out about the selection process for juniors that wanted to go to the World Championships to represent Canada. Surprisingly, I got a quick response in the form of a letter that told me in general that my son needed to accomplish standards which were very close to world records as part of the criteria. If he did that my son would be responsible for all costs of going to the world championships. I never had a problem standing up for my riders in the past, but I felt uncomfortable bragging about my son. I did it for so many years for other riders and I was sick of it. After a lot of thinking I called my own club in Poland and then I signed him up with the Polish Cycling Federation. It was not a problem since he had a dual passport. Cycling was big in Poland and there were hundreds of juniors and lots of races through the summer compared to only a dozen juniors at the most in Ontario. I did not know why but in Canada the selection process was too difficult. In Poland It was simple despite hundreds more juniors and all financial support being covered by clubs and the federation. It had not changed much since I raced many years before. If anyone wanted to be a world champion at the end it made no difference what country they were from.

Looking back, it seems some people did not want Peter racing for Canada, which is bizarre given the fact that he was incredibly strong for his age. Everyone had heard of him and his dominance. They all knew my son as he had never lost a race in Quebec. He was winning over 30 races a year in all categories by the age of 16 in the US and Canada. As soon as he finished school in Canada, I bought him a plane ticket to Poland where his grandparents would take care of him and drive him to all of his races and cheer him on. The club coaches would take him to the bigger races for the summer with the rest of the team. Eventually in 1998 at the age of 16 he became the Polish junior champion. His hard work paid off and he got on the Polish National Team. Everything happens for a reason, so maybe it was for the best.

Ever since I was a very young boy, I've always challenged myself to be stronger. I would train on my bike even after workouts were finished. I trained when everyone else had gone home for the day. Some people have that drive and self-motivation to push themselves, others need friends and fellow teammates to drive and inspire them. Choosing one's peer group is very important and I depended on mine for support. There was some truth in my father Boleslaw saying, "with whom you hang around, that's who you become".

Later in life the biggest motivator for my family in Canada was poverty. That is to say, moving up the financial ladder as soon as possible as there is really no other way. As a coach I worked harder and longer hours than any other coach and people took notice from the beginning. I regularly took dozens of athletes in a van across the United States for warm weather camps and to big international races. I did this to make my kids better athletes and to support them during competitions. I was the only one crazy enough to do it.

On one occasion I got a surprise compliment from national team coach Ron Hayman, the great ex-pro, who was at one point, the king of criteriums in America. We were at the first ever level three coaching certificate seminar in Victoria for three days. One of the subjects we discussed were provincial and national coaches. Ron said in front of everybody that I was the most efficient coach he had ever seen and I never wasted energy and time on something that was not important. Later that evening at the bar, Ron gave me another compliment: he said he wished when had started cycling he had me as a coach, he had no doubts he would have been much better. In his day, training was old school: no hills in winter, and flat rides in fixed gears. He knew of my training methods and of their success. It was a huge compliment from such an accomplished rider and former Canadian national coach.

24

In 1999, I went back to my private coaching business, which included training camps and personal training programs. That spring, at the age of 16, my son won his first pro race in Yuma, Arizona and he earned $2500 in prize money. At the same criterium, I borrowed a bike and asked the race organizer if they would let me race without a license in any category. They told me I could buy a one-day license and choose my own category. I paid all the fees and entered the masters/senior Category Three. I hadn't been on my bike in a week since I had been coaching my team at the Redlands Stage Race. To my joy, I beat the pack and not only won "solo" the race but earned $600 for my effort. One rider from California protested but his argument was very weak. Since I was an unknown and he never seen me before he assumed I was a Category One (highest category) rider and therefore should not have been in the Master category race. I had to convince them I was not a Cat One racer by showing them my hairy legs, (a true racer always had shaven legs), and the borrowed bike. In the end I lost the argument, the medal and the $600. I don't think the organizers knew my ability when they told me to enter any category I wanted. In the end, I was happy that my 16-year-old son got $2500.

Later that year in Verona, Italy at the world championships, Peter was in the winning breakaway group in the road race, riding with future world pro champion Fabian Cancellera of Switzerland. As luck would have it, his tire developed a slow leak and toward the end of the race he fell behind the break. Despite that, with his consistent results on both continents winning over 30 races a year in the past 2 years, he received two contract offers from teams in the USA. One was from Greg Avon and his senior team the Kissena Team and the other from Tobi Stanton of Hot Tubes junior team which offered total of $15,000. So Peter at 17 years old will race junior races with Hot Tubes, and senior races for Kissena.

The year 2000 did not start well for me. My father passed away after refusing to go to the hospital. All my family came together for the funeral. I was already in Poland taking part as a manager of the Hot Tubes team that came from the US to do European races. It was a sad occasion, but he lived a long, good life and he raised good offspring.

After a month-long training camp in Tucson AZ, I started seeing results from my athletes. Peter won the first race of the year, called the Valley of The Sun and Aron Carter won the senior women category. It was a good test for a 17 year-old racing in the senior category, as he prepared for his European races. Peter's main goal was to win the UCI Junior World Cup that year. Most of the races were in Europe, and the winner was determined by how many points were accumulated over the course of the ten different events. Winning the World Cup was statistically impossible for Canadians, no one from Poland or Canada had ever won this prestigious title in the junior category.

The first World Cup race was in Poland. I met with the Polish coaches before the race and made a pact that we would make sure every stage would be won by a Polish racer. That Hot Tubes racers wouldn't chase down Polish national team riders, and so on. It all started very well until Peter unexpectedly won the first stage and became the leader. There was a lot of controversy. I ended up in a fight with all the Polish coaches. Peter was racing with the Hot Tubes team, No one had a problem with that before the races, but when Peter became the leader, the Polish coaches suddenly didn't like this. It may have been different if he had been wearing the Polish national team jersey, but he was wearing the American Hot Tubes kit.

So the next day in Stage Two, the Polish national team riders combined with the Russians and attacked on the second stage and there was not much we could do. At the end, two Russians and one Polish national team member made a breakaway and Peter dropped to fourth place. I felt tricked by the Polish national team and to add insult, they joined with Russians to beat us? Man, I was mad.

On the third day the stage was long and windy. During the race, one of the Polish racers got a flat tire and all Polish national team riders stopped to get him back into the peloton during some very strong winds. As soon as this happened I told my boys to put the hammer down with the Russians and the Germans this time and so the Polish riders didn't make it back onto the main peloton with their leader. The Russians won the race and we ended up winning the team general classification. Peter was third overall.

After the race the Polish coaches were furious about Peter and his team and my tactics. My simple defense was when Peter was the leader he did not count as a Polish rider, and was attacked and ended up losing the entire race.

The next races, in Holland, Belgium and Germany, Peter finished top three. Peter next entered the most prestigious World Cup race of them all, the Peace Race. He won two stages there and general classification by only one second.

His success continued as he became the top Canadian/Polish racer and won the biggest North American stage race the Tour of l'Abitibi as well, taking the overall World Cup title.

The last big race of the year was the World Championships in France. My son did not have much left in his legs. His racing season started in Arizona in February, and now it was October and after 80 races he was exhausted. Even though Peter had not lost an individual time trial all year, the Polish team was sure he would win the race and started celebrating a week before. Peter was in a difficult position, physically exhausted showing poor form on the bike. He rode the rollers for most of the time, as it was too tiring to ride on the road. It was cold, rainy and windy in Brittany, France in October. He only rode the TT course twice and very slowly as it was very hilly with technically difficult and challenging roads.

On race day it started snowing in the morning. Snowflakes on rollers! I've never seen a rider warming up on rollers and snow coming down. Peter was to ride second last, with the lucky number "two" on his back. All the participants started one minute apart. By the time Peter got to line the snow had stopped. It was still very cold, windy and wet. Despite having his tire blow on his disc wheel moments before racing, Peter was in a total state of total concentration. He had junior gears, which meant they were special, restricted gears so young riders would not push too hard and injure their knees. It also meant it was hard to get a wheel with proper junior gearing. At the end they found disc wheels with junior restriction gears, but the bad news was it had a 18 mm track tire which was suited to smooth and perfect surfaces. This non threaded tire was certainly not suited to the rough and slippery roads that he was racing. Peter never lost composure, he just focused on the race ahead of him. He took off his heart rate monitor and told me not to say anything from the car.

It was incredible to see my son at age 17 not giving up his dream and trying to execute the race of his life despite all the mishaps and exhaustion in his legs. It was to be an epic race. He started slowly for the first 100 meters and once he had cleared the small town he opened up and rode full speed into the strong winds which were gusting from every direction. At the checkpoint before the first climb of the 21 km course, the helicopter began flying above us. I knew this was a good sign since in the Tour de France the helicopter followed winners so we knew things were good. The radio told us that Peter was leading with the fastest time on the first time check. I rolled down the window and told him the good news as it was a great motivator. He rode up the last two hills in the biggest junior gears he had. The last two kilometers were downhill to the finish. I never expected that he would pull it off, given his sensations in his legs prior. Listening to the Polish national anthem, the greatest Polish song, was a priceless experience. Right after the race, the number one pro team in the world, MAPEI, came to sign my son for a three-year contract. It's funny to note that the team manager had approached Peter just before the race when he was training on his rollers, and he'd told him he was busy. Peter signed the contract after the race and became financially secure in his own right.

25

The new century started very well for my private business of coaching. I had athletes from all over the world asking for coaching services, so I became very busy. After my usual training camp in Tucson it was time for my son to go to Europe. And his career started to take off since he had a contract with the best team in the world. Everything was falling into place, but as soon as he got to Europe he experienced knee pain. After some X-rays, it was determined that he required surgery. It was a condition he was born with but tolerated for many years. While departing Europe for surgery, my son was arrested at the airport. It was crazy. In Warsaw, he had been paying for things with travelers checks which turned out to be flagged by the Visa. The numbers on the checks we bought from the bank were misprinted. The VISA representatives came to the airport jail to rescue him, since it was their mistake to sell travelers checks with bad numbers. He didn't need a lawyer and Visa reimbursed him generously for their mistake.

So the problem was properly fixed and quickly went away.

Peter then flew to Canada for surgery, but of course the problem with Canada was that although surgeries were free, sometimes waiting for them would take forever. Through some old connections, I found the name of a doctor in Massachusetts who specialized in knee surgeries. He was one of the best in North America; a former hockey captain with the Hartford Whalers. We knew we were in good hands because his confidence was infectious. In five days and many US dollars later, Peter's knee was fixed and were driving back to Dundas. It took a while for the knee to be ready for punishment. He had the surgery in May and a few short months later he was winning the biggest one day race in Canada, the 250-km long Quebec-Montreal race.

One late afternoon I had a knock on my door. In front of me was an older bald man with a scar on his face. He did not know but it was his lucky day as I was in a good mood. Normally I did not like unknown people coming to my house. He told me he had heard about me and wanted to hire me as his coach. When I started my private coaching I never turned away anyone over age 15. To this day I don't believe in coaching very young people for cycling, under 15 they should be riding for fun, and playing other sports. There's no reason for training plans. That is how my son grew up, doing cross-country, soccer, and basketball, winning titles for his school. I never told him what to do. I felt sorry for children whose parents pushed them to do things that seemed to be more of their parents' dreams than theirs.

The man at the door was named Fred. He was in his '40s. and was a master rider who just started riding a year earlier without much success. He had a scar on his face. I assumed the scar on his face was from a cycling accident as many cyclists, myself included, had scars all over our bodies. It took a year of knowing him and to learn about where he got his scar. I never asked, as I figured he would tell me. It took a year of knowing him to find out how he got it.

The scar was not from bike-related surgeries but from a brain tumor surgery. I discovered later that Fred had overcome many challenges in his life. Years earlier when he found out his wife was pregnant, everyone kept asking him if it was going to be a boy or girl to which his answer was that it didn't matter, as long as it was healthy. Labor was long, 23 hours, but soon he was the proud father of a baby boy. The next thing he knew, the doctor was taking him aside to give him some bad news, his first boy had Down's Syndrome. At first he didn't believe it but a moment later his wife burst into tears. The experience of raising Sam through the years showed the strength of his dedication and family.

When Sam was five years old, Fred started experiencing ringing in his ears. After some tests the prognosis was acoustic neuroma. He endured a long surgery where doctors opened his skull and removed a golf ball–sized tumor. A surgeon had botched the surgery, leaving the left side of his face paralyzed. On one side of his face, his eye never closed. His facial nerves had been cut and half his face was paralyzed for the rest of his life. It was something he learned to live with, simple as that. But he was also very dedicated, as I would soon learn.

While recovering from surgery, Fred experienced big problems with balance and decided the best way to recover was to start exercising, to get fit and become a champion in cycling. Under my coaching, Fred started to train very hard. He did not have much choice. In cycling, it's very hard to gain respect, and the only way to do it is to win races or win group rides. In the first year of his training with me, he entered the masters 40+ National Championships, and to my surprise, lost only to Olaf Stanna from B.C. Stanna was an absolute icon in master's cycling, so it was a very good ride for Fred.

After that respectable result, a lot of local riders started to ask him about his training. This was the same year that riders from my program won three medals at the National Canadian Championships: Mark Walters, Duncan Gavin and Fred.

A big surprise was Duncan. His former coach had told him he lacked talent so he moved to Dundas from Vancouver to be coached by me. After living in Ontario and doing the training he needed, he ended up at the top of the podium, first place in the time trial at the nationals. It was a rewarding trip seeing my riders do so well. But Fred's accomplishment that stood out the most for me. He started cycling late in life because he wanted to get fit and lose weight. I don't think he ever expected he would go on to be a champion. Overtime, Fred became my closest friend. Mark was a comeback kid, winning the pro race. I was very happy for him winning his 3rd road race Canadian title.

26

Before his big win, Mark had already been back training with me for a few years. Under me, five years earlier, he had been crowned Canadian Junior Champion. The first priority in endurance sports is to build a strong base on which confidence can be developed. Mark's first test of confidence under my guidance was the early season race, the Niagara Classic. It was a very challenging race with 12 repeats of the famous Effingham Loop. During a conversation about tactics the night before, I encouraged Mark to get ahead and ride solo to prove that his talent was way above the others. He liked the idea and the next day he won the race using this strategy. The solo win gave him a confidence boost which he really needed. In 2002 Mark would win the biggest one-day race in America, the USPRO Championships. He was only Canadian to ever do that! The USPRO Championships was an incredible race with a rich history held every year in Philadelphia. Hundreds of thousands of people would gather to watch it, always on a hot sunny day in June. The pro men would ride 250 km on a very tough course, with two big hills. The first, was the most famous, Manayumk, and it was lined with a ton of drunken, excited fans. It looked very much like a big pro race in Europe. And it sort of was, all the best teams in Europe would come to race against the top American teams. Mark won by out sprinting a small break of 11 that was holding off a top-notch field. It was the biggest win of his career, and he did it in absolute style. Not only did he win the American National Championships, but he did so in a Canadian National Championship jersey! Just incredible.

Sometimes it's hard to believe and understand the human psyche. Working hard to achieve the goals is the most important part of being successful at anything we set our mind to. The other part of making dreams come true is to believe in the work we do.

In 2003, Mapei Team stopped their long existence, Peter's pro contract with Team Mapei was not renewed and he was quite disappointed. At the time, it was ranked the top team in the world and he had enjoyed many years of success under its sponsorship. So in 2003, while still recovering from knee surgery and not in top riding shape, he had to find a new team. He was working hard to return to his old form and started to show results in the Tour of Poland where won the best young rider jersey. Next, he came 15th at the u-23 World Championships.

Sport is difficult and high pressure at the pro level as you're only as good as your last result. Getting a contract is based on your wins and race performances, not on your potential talent. No one feels sorry for anyone, it is cruel and simple. That's why the only ones who survive and become pro are the ones not only with talent but tough personalities and commitment.

27

In 2002 Toby from Hot Tubes asked me if I would be interested in coaching a 15-year-old girl who was showing potential. Since Toby had a good eye for talent and a budget for her development, it was an easy decision. Her name was Larssyn Staley, a tall girl from Portland, Oregon. Toby sent her up to Canada for four weeks so I could meet her and adjust her bike position. All athletes coached by me during my career had to sit on a bike according to my eyes. I could not work with someone not sitting properly according to my philosophy. I was always very picky about it and would not work with anyone not sitting properly according to my methods. It was important to me. Another reason Larssyn came to Canada was so I could learn more about her, her abilities and limits. That year as a cadet, she won the nationals in every event she entered.

A year later I escorted her to Europe for some good caliber races and to prepare her for her first junior world championships taking place in Germany. In her first championships, Larssyn came sixth, seconds off the medal winning pace of 42.5km/h. It was a good sign as she was only 16 and had one more year in the junior category.

One very unusual thing about Larssyn was she was never homesick which meant I saw her in training more often through the year. She never missed training camps and worked hard for the 2003 season with the rainbow jersey on her mind. 2003 was a special year for cycling in my town Hamilton. The Canadian Nationals and World Championships were coming to town and it was hard to believe that all the best in the world would be competing there. First were the Canadian Nationals that were organized as a testing ground three months before the World Championships.

It became a bit stressful for some of my riders to compete in front of friends and neighbors. The most nervous was Fred. He had his reasons. The individual time trial course climbed up the Hamilton escarpment for one and a half kilometers and went right through his neighborhood at the top of the hill. This hilly loop was repeated twice. The racecourse was technically challenging, running through city streets with sharp corners. Since Fred was new to cycling he was not good technically. Most of the time trials he raced in the masters category were straight out and back. He never mastered racing up steep hills either. It was just not his thing. On top of that his neighbors would be sitting on the grass top of escarpment watching him going by and suffering. They had watched Fred cycle by over the years, oblivious to the pain and suffering he endured as a competitive athlete.

The stress of his neighbors watching him race was not Fred's only issue. Three days before the race while motor-pacing, Fred crashed on his bike. His time trial bike was damaged beyond repair so he was out of a bike for the race. Luckily his bike position and size was much the same as mine so I lent him my bike. I used my bike for local races and never rode against my athletes in championship events. That was part of my philosophy.

Fred's anxiety and apprehension going into the race was growing and he needed a confidence boost. Personally, I didn't know how he was going to ever get up the two hills on my bike and with his neighbors watching him suffer. Two days before the race, I came up with an idea. I asked my wife to bring home a bunch of colored pills, which were actually vitamins but looked quite impressive.

On race day, after Fred had almost finished warming up on my bike just a few minutes before the scheduled start of his TT, I asked him to follow me behind a big garbage container. As soon as we got there I told him to open his hands and I gave him the pills. I showed him the pills and told him that they were from Europe and were the best stuff on the market. As he was so nervous about his race, he never questioned what he was doing and swallowed the pills. I had a hard time keeping a straight face. Right after, he took his TT bike and went to the start line. Ten meters into the race, he dropped his chain and at that point I thought he'd never make it to the finish line. Thirty minutes later to everybody's surprise Fred won the Nationals in the 40+ age category by two seconds. After the race he told me that the pills were incredible and asked if he could buy some more. My answer was brief, I told him they were hard to obtain and were very expensive. With all the odds against him, I am still amazed at what he accomplished that day. Ten years later, I told him about the pills and we had a good laugh. For me as a coach, it was one of the funniest experiences in my coaching career.

In recent years it has become popular for athletes and celebrities to portray themselves as victims and bend the facts or to embellish them to gain attention and empathy from the public or their sponsors. Rather than take responsibility for their own actions, be it drug or alcohol addictions or self-imposed mental issues they often blamed the system, their parents or coaches. Most of them had no real understanding of true victims of poor mental or physical health, poverty or abuse or global conflicts. Some would even throw their own family members and friends under the bus to gain attention and pity. However, in the long run, most people find out the truth and the fame fades away with time.

The year 2003 was nearing its end and so was the racing season. The World Championships were to take place in Hamilton in October. I was looking forward to the races as my riders had good shots to do well, especially the three riders who had proven themselves in international competition. For the second time in my coaching career, I had athletes from three different countries participating. Sue Palmer had been top-ten at the Olympics before, and of course I had my son Peter, and Larssyn Staley who was declared World Champion in the junior points race a few months earlier. I was also cheering for three of my ex riders that came out from mine development program. I had someone to cheer for in every event. The whole cycling world was coming to town, including fans from many countries. The weather was good, it was warm with no rain in over a week.

However, for my athletes, it was not meant to be. They had a string of bad luck. Peter had barely trained in the three weeks leading up to the races because of an iron deficiency and ended placing 15th. Larssyn was plagued with mechanical issues in the time trial which cost her a medal and landed her in ninth place. And finally Sue finished a disappointing 13th in the pro women's road race. We had worked hard that year to prepare for this event but some things are hard to control and you have to accept it. We could have had two medals if things went perfectly, but that is part of sport. Nothing comes easy. Just like life, not everything happens the way we plan but luckily there is always next year. We have to move on and plan to do better and hope for some luck next time.

For me, Larssyn's title on the track was the one to remember. She was the third rider to come out of my program and become a world champion. And It did not come easy. We spent a lot of time training together that year, attending training camps and entering many races. In 2003, in the final four weeks leading up to the Junior World Championships in Moscow, we trained at the velodrome in Portland, Oregon. Since Larssyn was on a limited budget, we did not have much choice. For most coaches it would have been a big problem to train there as it is an old outdoor concrete velodrome, and we would be racing in a fast, indoor velodrome for the world championships. Secondly, the Moscow velodrome had a smooth wood surface where many records had been set. The Portland track, on the other hand, had a bumpy concrete surface and lots of wind coming from the ocean. On top of that the size 268 m (250m is standard) and the very steep banking and sharp turns were making the track much slower. Ideally a coach would choose to train on a surface that simulated the race in as many ways as possible for the rider to get familiar with the surface, angles, wind and the length of the track, which help timing and performance. As a coach, I had mixed feelings about the whole thing but with the track choice out of my hands, keeping Larssyn positive and confident was number one on the list. Creating a challenging training plan that would garner results was number two. I encouraged Larssyn to focus on her goals and to train three times a day. It took three years of hard training to get her to where she was now so she could tolerate a lot of training and had no problems with recovery. The best part of the program was that some days we'd go for the third ride of the day, for two hours and end up stopping at a golf course and pigging out on incredible blackberries, which grow everywhere in Portland. The main training session was on the velodrome. I tried to use a motorcycle as much as possible to simulate the speed on the indoor track. It was not easy. The ocean wind never stopped, and the surface was a concrete track. Ten days before the championships, I started to ease off the program. Larssyn, only 17, was getting very tired physically, but mentally, she was good and her legs started to open and unblock.

She left for Moscow feeling satisfied with her form, confidence and speed. First time on the Moscow velodrome with the US national team her sensations were positive. She called me after her first day riding on the track with the American team. She said that after Portland, she felt like she was riding downhill. Now the only worry was choosing the proper gearing for her strength and fitness. I was feeling very optimistic, the winds of Oregon and the old outdoor track had done their job.

The first race of the championships was the points race: one rider per country racing at the same time accumulating points every ten laps for 40 laps. After a long battle and aggressive racing, Larssyn was leading the race coming into the final sprint. Her hard training paid off, and despite crashing at 60 km/hr on the last turn of the track before the finish, she quickly got up and grabbed her broken bike and ran to the finish line. Incredibly, she had accumulated enough points to win the world championships crossing the finish line running.

Afterwards, doctors in the hospitals advised her not to race anymore in those championships, as she had a concussion and lots of bruises. She had the potential to win the two kilometer pursuit but we will never know how she would have done. Life and cycling had made her strong and her hard work ethic transferred to real life. She could always count on herself. Later on in life she left for Europe on her own, earned her PHD and became a professor in Switzerland. Many things cannot be taught, we are born to be fighters, not afraid to try things on our own, not afraid of taking risks in life. Some people never want to follow their dreams as they are too afraid of failure or just plain lazy.

28

For the 2004 Summer Olympics, I only had one rider from my program, Sue Palmer, competing. She wanted to end her career with the Olympics. Since I had moved to Dundas in 1991, Sue had been part of my program. Strangely she's the only rider with whom I never had a disagreement. First time I heard about Sue Palmer was in Calgary where my Manitoba women's team took part in a big stage race which she won. When I moved to Dundas I found out Sue was attending McMaster University and living only five kilometers from me. As soon as my program started, Sue was there taking part in our training camps and the local daily group rides. It took a long time to learn her story, since she was not one to talk about her past.

Sue was from Collingwood and her first encounter with sport was at the age 12, when she started skiing with the school team. Her ski coach, who was a teacher, was looking for kids who owned skis and found out from her father that she had a pair. The first couple of years she trained with the school team and did not show much potential. It all changed when her biggest supporter, her father passed away, with heart problems. She was 16 years old when she changed and became fanatical about her training. She also started recording her training in journals and soon was winning ski races. She began setting goals: not how she would win but by how much.

One year, there was a cycling race organized for citizens in her town. Her friend loaned her a bike and clothing to race a 20 km race for novice riders. It took some time for her mom to buy her first bike since she was taking care of five kids, and money was tight. Sue was hooked on cycling and she started riding every day. Sue's sporting career was to include biking in the summer, and skiing in the winter. Sports motivated her to work harder and to do something her father wanted her to do.

There was always a shortage of money but that didn't stop her. She was more motivated than ever and committed to doing well in the sport of cycling. Eventually, she had to make a choice: either three exams at university, or attend a provincial team training camp in South Carolina. Her choice was training camp. She ended up having a remarkable cycling career representing Canada in both the 1996 and 2004 Olympics and was inducted into the Canadian Cycling Hall of Fame in 2018. Despite very little financial support from her family while growing up, she did the best she could and made it on her own, not only as an athlete but as a teacher and a loving mother of three children. She persevered through much of her life without a father and coaching her on and off for 14 years was an experience that set the benchmark for future female athletes. She pushed others in training and helped many to become better athletes. She represented Canada until 2006 when she raced her last World Championships.

In 2005 my coaching business progressively picked up from year to year. I started to have clients not just from the USA and Canada but from Europe and Asia as well. Some of my well-off clients decided to form a cycling club called Mazurcoaching. They raised the money to get it rolling. It meant more work for me including ordering clothing, spending money on projects and completing administrative tasks. But I agreed to do it to support the young riders for the future of cycling. The master riders ordered clothing with their name on the jersey. We received a lot of donations and I was not sure what to spend all the money on. By then, we had around 40 members. We raced in Europe and I started to organize trips to Belgium, Poland and the United States for much needed experience for European racing. We received free equipment from Radek at the Wheels of Bloor bike shop. On weekends, we traveled to bigger races in the US, and all our efforts began to pay off and we became the number one ranked club in Ontario.

Also in 2006, my son became the Polish national champion in the professional category for the second time. He also raced in the Giro d'Italia, the Tour of Poland, Tour of Germany, Tour of Britain and other big races like Paris-

Roubaix. Eventually he retired from cycling and started a clothing company, Kallisto. The company was selling in over 16 countries on five continents.

29

I opened my eyes and slowly realized I was in a very dark room in hospital. I had just undergone five hours of heart surgery. The big clock was clicking very loudly on the wall in the room. At the sometime something was clicking on the man next to me. But it was clicking at a faster pace. When he woke up I found out we both just had open heart surgery and replaced valves. The ticking I heard was the mechanical valve he had ended up with. Later he told me that he had suffered a heart attack early in the morning at work which was one hour away from the hospital. He was very lucky and it was obviously it was not his time to go. I had a hard time sleeping, due to his noisy carbon valve. I, on the other hand, had a pig valve implanted which was perfectly quiet. As my surgery was not an emergency, I had time to choose the type of valve I wanted. My chest was cut in half and I could taste the metal wire in my mouth for days after they sawed open my rib cage and then used wire to hold it together. I felt no pain at all but I was well drugged up.

My heart problems had begun years earlier. In 1996 before the Olympics. I experienced migraines from stress and one time I had to go to hospital since I started to vomit and I couldn't eat. I was lying in the hospital on the bed getting fed and hydrated through tubes for eight hours until an old doctor checked on me. The stress before the Olympics was starting to show. It's one thing to coach at the Olympics when you have no chance of podium finishes and it's another when five of your athletes are medal contenders. The stress was really getting to me and my competitiveness and sense of perfection did not help. I was taking sleeping pills in the evening and in the morning I would have three cappuccinos before I ate to wake up so I could function during training sessions. The doctor that came to do the check up put his hand on my neck and chest, and told me I had a heart problem and when I had a chance to go see a cardiologist. Weeks later after the many tests I got news that I needed open heart surgery immediately. The news was not good. Just the idea of my chest being opened wide and my heart not beating for three hours scared me. The whole procedure would take around five hours.

My heart seemed great at the time and I was riding my bike strong and felt very fit even winning races here and there. I was skeptical about my diagnosis so my wife found another cardiologist to get a second opinion. This was the best thing to do at the time since heart surgery is not a joke. The second doctor was originally from England and was considered the best cardiologist in Hamilton. He also happened to live in my neighborhood. He was old and had a very dry sense of humor with a British accent. At my first appointment he put his hand on my wrist and told me my heart was strong. He said it was good news. I was born with a heart murmur which runs in the family. I should not worry about it. He said no surgery was needed yet but he would monitor me yearly. Since my mother had the same condition and was 80 years old and still going strong, he figured I would never need it. It was great news before the Olympics since I was already stressed out to the maximum. One thing did not change, the awareness of my heart problem was always at the back of my mind especially when I raced or did heavy work.

Eleven years later, after one of the yearly check-ups, I finally got the news. My regular English cardiologist was on sick leave for four months after having a heart attack him self and there was a replacement doctor. The news came from the new doctor. I was not afraid and was mentally prepared despite having seen the entire procedure on video beforehand. During my first meeting with the surgeon I asked when he could do it. And to my surprise he said next week. I did not tell any of my clients about the surgery. On the day of surgery I felt good, even being funny and joking through the preparation process. The fun ended when I was rolled into the operating room. It had no windows and was cold. I expected maybe three people like I had seen on television yet there were at least eight people. I started to get scared, especially when they tied my arms to the surgery bed. The anesthetist that I had met with per-surgery interview was not there. In his place was a doctor from Africa who apologized for the other anesthetist who was supposed to be there. Next thing I knew I was recovering in the post-op room.

Most people stay in the hospital for five days after surgery, which is pretty routine. My nightmare started on the first day after a nurse gave me some painkillers. I had a bad reaction to them and I started vomiting a lot even after I did not eat. I was in tremendous pain as my chest heaved every time I vomited. It was not fun. I was trying to hold my rib cage and vomit at the same time thinking it would eventually open the wounds. My surgeon, who was a professor at McMaster, had left town and the nurse in charge would not listen to my wife (who is a pharmacist) who said to give me the painkillers intravenously, not orally. She continued to refuse to give drugs intravenously. After five days I had no energy to lift my head and only ate ice cubes. Finally my surgeon came back from a trip and ordered the nurse to change drugs to IV. By that point I was convinced I was going to die.

I started having nightmares all the time since I wasn't sleeping regularly. I was in hell and visited heaven in my constant nightmares. I started to feel disoriented where I was and if I was alive. The clock on the wall became louder and especially at night when it was very dark. The only light was coming from the hallway, from a little window in the metal door. After seven days in hell I lost 16 pounds and I did not care about anything anymore. It's hard to believe that 14day earlier I had been very strong and breaking cycling records on the local time trial. I looked like I was from a concentration camp. My wife had had enough. After eight days, she told the doctor she was taking me home. She said the food in the hospital wouldn't help me gain back the weight. Soon I was lying with not much life in me on the back seat of the car going home. It took some time for me to gain weight and become strong again.

After surgery I never felt my heart again and it was very quiet and working properly. Some weeks later I was strong enough to go to the Hamilton banquet to pick up my last ever trophy for the fastest time of the year. Looking back, what happened to me was bad luck, and very rare. Generally in Canada we receive excellent medical care, and world class surgeons.

30

In 2011 my son was looking to sponsor some riders who were not affiliated with any team and with his clothing. He came across a rider named Ania Harkowska, who was a para-athlete who also raced in the open category against able-bodied cyclists. Ania had no team at the time which made her a perfect candidate. Later on I found out she had been hit by a car while standing at a bus stop at age 22. She suffered 26 fractures and nearly lost her left leg. After numerous surgeries and months of rehab she switched from running to cycling. Soon she was strong enough to compete in all cycling events. When I heard her story I wanted to help her. My son connected me with her and I started to coach her, and in the first few months she trained in Poland. Then Peter bought her a ticket to Canada so I could finally meet her and help her to prepare for the upcoming Olympics. I always made sure my athletes did my program and my exercises the proper way, so meeting in person was important. This included precise adjustments to bike position and perfect execution of intervals since every heartbeat counts. In my opinion I could never develop an athlete to their best potential and get top results from just a phone conversation.

Canadian spring is not always warm, so at first Ania did a lot of training on the rollers, which helped me as a coach develop new ideas for training. After four weeks in Canada, her fitness and power dramatically increased and we started to discuss her goals, winning medals at the Polish regular able Championships.

She had already started winning at local time trials in Hamilton and on some training days she was holding speeds of 43.5km/h.

I made a decision to enter Ania into the biggest international competition in Canada with my Club Mazurcoaching. We traveled to Ottawa which was six hours away. After a grueling race, Ania was five seconds out of the top ten with 32 international top riders behind her. It was a great result especially since she had borrowed a bike from the Wheels of Bloor bike shop and the competition had included many past world champions. During the time she stayed with me, she started winning the Ontario Cup races. She even won the Hamilton Club TT and set a new record in the women's category. Weeks later Ania became the Polish National Champion and had a chance to wear the national champion jersey.

A year later Ania won a silver medal at the 2012 London Olympics in the Paralympic event. At all the races we attended together, she showed great spirit, never losing her composure and racing with enthusiasm and a smile plastered on her face. It was hard to believe that a person in her financial situation trying to survive on government funding and some small sponsorship never complained or gave up. While on the road, she constantly entertained and uplifted our inexperienced team. Her disability was never an excuse, her Olympic dream was her focus and was the goal.

Many people take their good health for granted. A positive attitude goes a long way in attaining success and achieving goals. No one can rely on raw talent, money or equipment alone; hard work and commitment are essential. You're only at 50 per cent without dedication. As a coach I helped people reach their full potential, winning medals and leaving it all on the road. I loved seeing my athletes win, it was addictive. Well, not a true addiction.

It is absolutely true that America is like no other place, the land of opportunity. Through hard work or luck, you could quickly become rich. But at the same time, you could lose it just as quickly if you hung around with the wrong people. Through the years I had clients who had come to America penniless and ended up rich on the Wall Street. One client was so wealthy he would fly me to his home just to adjust his seat position and he paid much more volunteerly than the rest of the riders for private coaching. I soon learned of his addictions and other problems and was glad to not have his lifestyle or millions. Money does not always buy happiness, it is the people we surround ourselves with that really influence our lives and who make us happy or sad. In any case, our decisions are our own and we can only blame ourselves for wrong decisions.

31

I've only had one addiction in my life and still do: obtaining vintage bikes. I got hooked at a winter training camp in Tucson. We were staying in very comfortable, fully furnished apartments that included a pool. On a hot sunny Arizona day, my athletes had the day off and were at the swimming pool. I did not go as I was never a big fan of swimming. At some point one of my riders came to my room and said that there was an old man at the pool who had bikes he wanted to get rid of. At first I thought it was a joke and the boys were trying to get me wet. Curiosity got the better of me and I went to check out the old man at the pool. The man I saw was in baseball cap, smoking a cigar and relaxing by the pool in a chair. He took us to his apartment and after waiting a few minutes at the door he came out with his old bikes. The bikes were very dirty from being stored outside on the balcony for months. He had three steel bikes and was asking $1000. I recognized the bikes immediately, high end bikes from 30 years ago. What a find! Of course I downplayed my enthusiasm and said I'd take all three off his hands for $500 as they were old, in bad shape and I had no use for them. He had a nice Italian Colnago which he said I could have for $200 and two of my riders offered $300 for the other two bikes. The Colnage was a little dirty, but it had never really been ridden so all it needed was a little clean-up. And it was my size. The old man accepted the offer and then I became suspicious that they might be stolen. I asked him straight up if he had stolen the bikes from a collector. The man went back to his apartment for a moment and brought out pictures from years earlier and told us his story. 25 years earlier he had been a millionaire, drove a Ferrari and bought lots of expensive toys. He had obtained the bikes at a bike show directly from the bike companies. He used to live in Manhattan. He had become addicted to drugs and consequently lost his Wall Street job and his fortune. He ended up moving to Tucson with his bike collection, his cigars and his addiction. He was selling his bikes as he needed the money. So we paid him and that day I started my collection of vintage bikes.

When we got back to the apartment, we were able to inspect the bikes more closely. I ended up with a 1984 Colnago Arabesque with a 50th anniversary Campagnolo Gruppo. That bike would have only been used for the bike shows or in a showroom. It was the top of the line flagship frame from a prestigious bike company and the best show bike at the time. One of my riders opened up his computer and I was introduced to eBay.

It was amazing, it was like the whole world was on eBay, all the collectors. My riders sold their bikes for $3000 each which covered their cycling experience for the entire year. My bike was another story. It was in another league. Its production was limited and the value was $7000 or more. I got attached to my Colnago quickly, I could not sell it. Over a decade, my collection grew from one bike to 75 bikes. The funny and ironic part of the story is that I got my addiction from another addict and the only part was that it was not drugs but bicycles which made me money. I believe everyone needs a hobby, something that can preoccupy our minds and help escape sometimes the reality of life. For me, it's collecting bikes.

One day I received an unexpected email from Ed Beamon. He was the manager at the time of one of the best teams in the USA, the Navigators. He knew me for many years, and that I was a no nonsense kind of guy. Our paths had crossed many times when I was coaching one of his best riders, Mark Walters. In 2002 he won the biggest one day race, the US Pro Championships in Philadelphia. Peter raced for him briefly as well, winning races in Europe before he signed a contract with the top professional team, Saunier Duval. In general we had mutual respect for each other. In the email, he asked if I could assess an unknown rider from Cuba. He was a new immigrant who didn't speak English, but his American wife did. The rider's name was Luis Amaran and according to Ed, he had great potential, but was not winning races and needed my help to take him to the next level. The strange part was the Cuban rider was on an opposing team and had nothing to do with Ed. I had only visited Cuba once for the Pan Am Games and one thing that stayed with me forever was the morning training on the roads during the games. My team would ride on the straight road that seemed like a Canadian highway, with the difference being that people were riding bikes and mopeds on it. What stuck in my memory was the kids riding city bikes in sandals and running shoes but not just riding to school. What was remarkable was that they were using heavily loaded trucks for motor-pacing and they repeated this twice a day. I could see 10 to 20 kids behind a truck, at 40km/h. I remember thinking about coaching in Cuba and all the potential talent in those riders behind the trucks riding in sandals.

I have visited many countries and I had seen lots of poverty but poverty in communist Cuba was different. In Cuba I never noticed rich Cubans driving expensive cars, I never saw poor people begging for money. It seems that most Cubans were on the same poverty level but not poor enough to beg on the streets. At the same time they had coupons for food but the grocery stores were empty. So when Ed contacted me, my dream came true. I had a first time chance to coach Cuban athletes. I never heard of

Luis before but according to Ed he had hidden potential and he was a hard working man who was a professional.

My biggest problem would be that he would not understand me and misinterpret my specific sense of humor that often took years for some athletes to get used to. Soon we were introduced, and the first thing we did was go through his past training years. I learned as much as I could and slowly introduced my way of coaching. At first it was strange. I gave Luis his first training plan and since he didn't speak much English, there was not much to discuss. If he ended up with any questions his wife would email me. Sometimes I had to change Luis' plan due to weather conditions. He lived in Albuquerque, New Mexico and sometimes there was snow as it was a town at high altitude. After five months on my program the first race of the season was coming and it was a big test for us. He placed second overall and in the top three in every stage In the three-day race, the Valley of The Sun. I knew I had a winner and 2010 looked promising. That year Luis, the Cuban immigrant, won the NRC, or National Racing Calendar challenge. His resume started to grow. It was strange some way we did not talk much but some athletes are so professional all they needed was the better program that would bring out their talent and make them stronger to start winning races.

I coached Luis until the end of his professional career and after winning many races during that time the only regret was that I never coached him from a young age. It was very gratifying to coach a kid similar to the ones I had witnessed riding behind the trucks pacesetters in Cuba so many years before. Luis had left Cuba for a better life and to fulfill his dream and I rate coaching him as one of my top accomplishments. Most people do not know that. I felt close to him because we both shared the immigrant experience.

As an immigrant you quickly learn to start saving money and in general how to do it efficiently on a limited budget. That means not wasting anything. As a young person I learned through my own mistakes as I never had anybody to guide me. The best way to learn is through the wisdom of others, those that have lived through it all before you. Everyone makes mistakes. At the age of 50, my family and I owned several properties both in Canada and elsewhere, and we still had hobbies and a nice life. The most fun part of it was that now, after all these years, the bank was our friend and borrowing money was never an issue. Things can change, I guess. Especially when you have money.

32

Over the Fall I was contracted by the Toronto Wheelchair Club president to ask if I was still coaching. I of course said yes, I was. He asked me if I would be interested in coaching a young man who had been in a car accident and had become a wheelchair athlete. I quickly said no, I had no interest or experience with that part of the sport. The president kept insisting and asked me if I could meet the rider once and make a decision. The next thing I knew, the future prospect was emailing me. I remember it was an early winter day, we had snow and slush, and it was windy. I was waiting at Café Domestique in Dundas. Anthony Lue called me saying he'd be late due to the road conditions. Twenty minutes later, I came out of the coffee place a bit upset, waiting for my new date to show up. Next thing I see a young black man rolling his wheelchair through the parking lot in the slush and snow. I could not believe that he had such determination on this cold, miserable day. If I had been him, I would more likely have been home watching TV. In order to get into the coffee shop, Anthony required a ramp but I didn't see one. I had been frequenting the cafe for years and never knew that there was a ramp out back. It's interesting the things you don't notice when you are able-bodied. We ordered coffee and had a general talk about past training. Anthony somehow convinced me to try and coach him. At the end we agreed to coaching fees and we set up a plan for the whole year. First off, just like all my other athletes, Tucson was in the plan. I always wanted to see my riders biking as much as possible early in the year as part of my program.

Anthony ended up having good indoor preparation before we went to Tucson. Generally athletes stayed in my Tucson house for the month. I had no ramp or a shower to accommodate wheelchairs so he had to stay at a hotel five kilometers away. The hotel was very expensive, $3000 a month. I never had a chance to talk about his financial situation but we agreed it would be better if he ate lunch and dinner prepared by me at my house. Soon I discovered that Anthony had no income and very little money; his friends were helping him through organizing events to fundraiser for his racing wheelchair and trips. On top of that he lived in a Toronto apartment in a sketchy neighborhood. However the logistics of the camp in Tucson looked to be an easy task for us, at first. But then it certainly was not. Very quickly I learned the difficulties and obstacles that wheelchair athletes face. Every day I drove five kilometers to the hotel. I had to put his racing bike in the back of my Dodge Caravan and then put him in the seat, then take his wheelchair into my car and we were ready to go. Upon arriving at my house I had to take his wheelchair out so Anthony could get in my house, then after we ate we drove to Mount Lemmon to start the training session. At the bottom of the big mountain, I again had to unload the wheelchair, and the racing bike and after Anthony was ready to train on his racing bike I put his wheelchair back in the car. After training was over I would do the same process, but in reverse. I always tried to cook dinners the day before so we didn't have to wait long after training. As soon as I found out about Anthony's financial situation I stopped charging him for coaching. He was such a proud man that for a long time he didn't want to tell me he had no money. But I was happy as the great part of him being in Tucson was he could train outside a lot more, with all the open roads and perfect weather.

The dry hot climate reduced his aches and pains that had been bothering him. He was often in pain because of the accident. The first year he was in Tucson he was able to make it up Mount Lemmon to Mile 14 which is a challenge for many local riders. Three years later he made it to the top, a full 45 kilometers and a 10000 feet of climbing.

The best part for him was meeting new people. Due to his charming personality he was meeting new people on the rides all the time. He took part in some local races for wheelchair athletes and met some local students on scholarships. He decided to apply for a scholarship for himself at the University of Arizona. It offered sport scholarships to disabled athletes. Anthony was accepted on a full scholarship to the University of Arizona. Racing bikes was Instrumental in him receiving his scholarship. Having played even a small role in Anthony's life is one of the most inspirational things I have ever experienced.

I always joked with him, when I was loading his wheelchair and his racing bike in and out of the car every day, and sometimes I could see he felt a bit guilty, but I just kept telling him "Hey, don't worry! I am just doing this so I can get my ticket into heaven." We both laughed.

33

2 5 years after leaving Manitoba I got an email from a rider who took part in the old program, someone with whom I'd lost contact. The email said, "you probably did not remember me, but you used to coach me." His name was Dale Dunner. He told me he had quit cycling and went to flying school to become a pilot, and he had worked for Cathay Pacific for the past ten years. He wrote to me: "I am a pilot of a Boeing 747 and I cannot help but think that my experience racing bikes helped me get there. I remember you telling me that I should put 100% into something or not do it at all. Thank you for the life lessons. And if you don't remember me, I wanted to write about how your coaching went far beyond two wheels."

Of course I remembered Dale. He asked me to come along for one of his flying days training. We met at a little airport outside Winnipeg. When we got inside of the small two-seater plane, smoke began spewing from the engine just as we were going to fly. He said, no problem, we will fly a different one. The next one was the same, a real rust bucket. Dale told me don't worry, if the engine fails we can glide. That did not comfort me. We began flying very low and eventually, Dale said "hey, lets go land at Winnipeg International Airport. Just to touch down and then leave". I said, "fine, sounds cool. It's a nice airport", and he needed the practice. We neared the airport and prepared to touchdown when all of a sudden there was a giant 747 behind us! And the control tower started yelling at us over the radio. We did touchdown and then departed but from that day, I promised myself I'd never again go in a two-seater.

I always liked to follow my athletes after their sojourn in cycling and most of them don't know that. Looking back I am very proud that I coached many athletes who became successful adults. Setting goals and dreams and working hard to accomplish them is important not just in sport but in real life. For some It's okay not to have them or don't care where they end up. Most of my successful athletes had their goals set up before they stopped cycling and they pursued them during their cycling careers. Sometimes those goals need to be changed for different reasons and one should not be afraid of that.

I was never afraid of changing dreams. The best example was immigrating to Canada, instead of Australia. It is impossible to speculate what I would be doing and who I'd have met in Australia. Would I have become a cycling coach and made differences in people's lives? I will never know. Life is a funny thing, you can only do it once. So you never know what the other road would bring.

Every November on Sundays I organized training sessions on top of Sydenham Hill in Dundas, Ontario where I lived. Routinely through the years we worked on strength during that period of time by riding up it ten times. I always parked my car on top of the hill at the parking lot at the lookout so I could see the town of Hamilton and Dundas Park. One time, on a cold, windy day, there was one other white car parked there with one person inside. My athletes were riding up and down the hill, as usual. I had two wheelchair athletes and a couple of road riders doing interval repeats which took 15 minutes each. In the middle of the training I noticed strange behavior in the car, which was parked alone. There was some screaming and some crying. I went to the white car and there was a young woman in there. I asked her if she was okay. She said she was fine. The young girl was crying, saying there was no problem, so I walked away figuring she must have broken up with a boy at a party the night before.

Ten minutes later I peeked in to be sure, and saw her with a bottle of pills. I then realized something was terribly wrong. I was worried and went to find a phone in my car, but then decided to circle back and talk to her. At that time she was out cold. I used my cell phone and called the police. The ambulance showed up from the Dundas Fire Department in minutes. She was unconscious and they took her on a stretcher to the hospital. The police interviewed me and made a report. I never found out what happened to the girl that tried to kill herself with all those medications. But at least she ended up in the hands of the paramedics who could treat her quickly, before it was too late. I hope the scare was enough to make her stop from doing it again. I hope she did well in her second chance in life.

It always made me think not only of the choices we make in life but the serendipitous encounters we experience. If I had never left Poland I would never have moved to Vancouver, Winnipeg or Dundas. If I had not been on Sydenham Hill that morning, I may never have saved that girl. No one was usually on that hill on a Sunday morning, especially on a cold, windy day in November. That's why she went there, so no one would get in her way. But because of the funny way life works, I was there. I always hear people say, everything happens for a reason. Maybe, just maybe, they are right or was it just another coincidence in life.

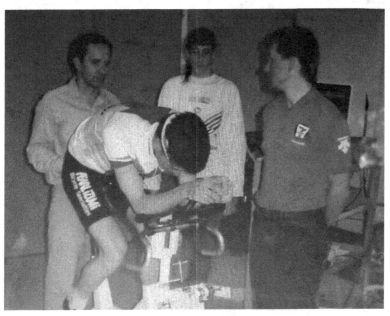

Testing at McMaster University with Bogdan and Sue

Pan-Am Games in Cuba, Tanya racing for gold

New innovation at work. Redesign Monark machine

With Brian at the Atlanta Olympics.

Taking brake from cycling

Back to coaching with Sue Palmer

Coaching USA National Team

Peter in action on one of the first made Cervelo bikes

Coaching next World Champion

Fred winning Nationals in Hamilton

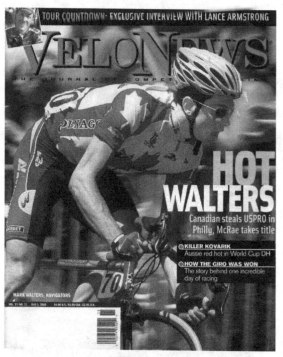

Mark Walters at his best

Peter on the podium at the World Championships in France

The start of my addiction

Building is always fun

Coaching Cuban Pro

My man Anthony and me

Winning three National Road Pro titles
in one year in three countries

Some people get second chance in life.
(on the top of Sydenham Hill)

Dinner with Prime Minister of Canada.

Athletes appreciation is always the best reward

Celebrating Cycling on the top of Sydenham Hill Climb

Epilogue

In 2010 I got an email from Cecilia Carter, a well known sports personality, former world record holder, Canadian champion, teacher and coach who was heavily involved in Canadian sport. I had never met Cecilia and was surprised with the email from her. In her email she introduced me to her idea of putting the plaque on the top of Sydenham Hill, at the lookout point, to celebrate the achievement of local cyclists. My first impression after reading her email was surprise, why would she put a plaque at the top of the hill and change its name after 100 years of history with the town? It seems she was very impressed by the accomplishments of the local cycling community over the years. However, changing the old name and getting the plaque was not easy. It took time and approval from the town, the local committees and politicians. Chris Hines, a local cycling enthusiast and the owner of Dundas Cafe Domestique, started fund- raising and a silent auction took place after the news spread around. I was the first to make a donation. I was very excited to have a cycling plaque placed atop a hill that I had used in training for over 20 years, developing cyclists into international stars.

During the time leading to April 27, 2013, I did not know the details of where and how everything would look at the end. As it happened, Cecilia did not disappoint, she organized a first

179

class event to celebrate cycling in my hometown of Dundas. It was a perfect sunny day and everything came together beautifully.

The ceremony started with many riders from the local clubs and out of town taking part in a parade biking slowly through town and ending the ride on the top of Sydenham Hill at the lookout point where I always stood timing my riders through the years when they were training. There were hundreds of people on the side of the road all the way cheering during the procession. At the lookout there was a plaque on a pedestal covered with black cloth. On arrival I could not believe who was in attendance. Some of Canada's greatest cyclists were there: Steve Bauer, Curt Harnett, Gord Singleton, Brian Shuter, Mark Walters, Sue Palmer and many other Olympians. Politicians from the government were giving speeches, with television cameras. The Hamilton mayor was present too and it was a great day to celebrate cycling. I received flowers from the young upcoming racers.

Even now, the climb is very popular with cyclists. On any given day you'll see young people doing intervals on it. I too try to ride there as much as I can. On some days, I marvel at everything that has happened since I moved here. I never would have dreamed the life I've been so lucky to live, the travel and people I've met, the races my riders have won, meeting the Prime Minister, going to the Olympics, seeing my riders become world and Olympic champions, changing people's lives.

That's why the Sydenham climb is so special to me. It's not just a one kilometer long hill. It's a place where dreams have come true, for riders, and for me. I saw an article a few years ago about how Dundas had become a mecca for cycling. And it's true, so many good riders had moved there to fulfill their dreams as bike racers. So I was thrilled when Cecilia explained the plaque would be there permanently in a big rock.

When it was time to remove the black cloth and unveil the plaque, it took a while for my wife and I to see it. It was made of bronze metal and looked heavy. It was painted black with gold letters. After reading the first sentence, all I saw was my name Coach Mirek Mazur !. I was shocked and felt proud of myself at the same time. All I can say, I wish my mother and father could have witnessed the ceremony and seen the solid metal plaque with my name placed on a big rock on top of the hill. I never dreamed that this could be possible that an immigrant who is still alive would get such recognition.

Celia never raced bikes but as a sports coach herself, appreciated all the hard work and dedication that it took to run a successful program on a small budget. Not to mention, all the obstacles that others thrown at you throughout the years. At age 50, I thought I achieved all my goals and dreams, but I kept coaching and doing what I do the best, helping the younger generation achieve their dreams and sometimes find their way in life.

Mirek Mazur
Dundas, Ontario.

Acknowledgments

There are many people I would like to thank that have been instrumental in my life. First of all, my mom Bronislawa, Aunt Staszka, Sister Josephine, Father John. Thank you to my inlaws, Babcia Lucynka and Diziadek Czesiek. Thank you to Jacob Heilbron, Jim O'Brien, and Colin Hearth. I need to also thank some of my athletes, Brian Walton, Susan Palmer-Komar, Mark Walters, Anthony Lue, Clara Hughes and Matt Hansen. I would also like to thank Kay Christie for her help all those years ago.

And of course, thank you to my wife Eva and son Peter.

Printed in the United States
by Baker & Taylor Publisher Services